OWNING THE FUTURE

About Policy Network

Policy Network is a leading thinktank and international political network based in London. We seek to promote strategic thinking on progressive solutions to the political, economic and social challenges of the 21st century, impacting upon policy debates in the UK, the rest of Europe and the wider world.

Policy Network organises debates and conducts research on policy and political challenges that present all governments and political parties with urgent dilemmas, either because sustainable solutions remain elusive or because there are political barriers to their implementation.

Through a distinctly collaborative and cross-national approach to research, events and publications, the thinktank has acquired a reputation as a highly valued platform for perceptive and challenging political analysis, debate and exchange—and as an unrivalled international point-of-contact between political thinkers and opinion formers, serving as a nexus between the worlds of politics, academia, public policymaking, business, civil society and the media.

www.policy-network.net

This publication would not have been possible without the support of Lord Bhattacharyya and WMG.

OWNING THE FUTURE

How Britain Can Make it in a Fast-Changing World

Edited by Chuka Umunna

}{ policy network

WMG
Innovative Solutions

ROWMAN &
LITTLEFIELD
INTERNATIONAL

London • New York

Published by Rowman & Littlefield International, Ltd.
16 Carlisle Street, London, W1D 3BT
www.rowmaninternational.com

Rowman & Littlefield International, Ltd. is an affiliate of Rowman &
Littlefield
4501 Forbes Boulevard, Suite 200, Lanham, Maryland 20706, USA
With additional offices in Boulder, New York, Toronto (Canada), and
Plymouth (UK)
www.rowman.com

British Library Cataloguing in Publication Information Available
A catalogue record for this book is available from the British Library

ISBN: PB 978-0-9928705-1-5

Library of Congress Cataloging-in-Publication Data

Owning the future : how Britain can make it in a fast-changing world / edited by Chuka
Umunna.
pages cm
ISBN 978-0-9928705-1-5 (pbk. : alk. paper) — ISBN 978-0-9928705-2-2 (electronic)
1. Great Britain—Economic policy—1997- 2. Economic development—Great Britain. I.
Umunna, Chuka, 1978–
HC256.7.O96 2014
338.941—dc23
2014030206

Printed in the United States of America

CONTENTS

ABOUT THE CONTRIBUTORS

Antonio Andreoni is a researcher in industrial economics and policy at the Institute for Manufacturing, Cambridge University, and coordinator of the Babbage Industrial Policy Network.

Billy Boyle is co-founder and president of Owlstone Nanotech Inc.

Ha-Joon Chang teaches economics at Cambridge University and writes a column for the Guardian. His last book *Economics: The User's Guide* was published by Penguin.

David Cleevely CBE is an entrepreneur who has founded a series of companies, including Abcam, Analysys, 3waynetworks and others. He also co-founded Cambridge Network, Cambridge Wireless, Cambridge Angels and the award-winning restaurant Bocca di Lupo, as well as acting as government advisor and founding the Centre for Science and Policy at the University of Cambridge.

Sherry Coutu CBE is an angel investor, entrepreneur and tech-investor, recently appointed to the board of the London Stock Exchange.

Lord Mervyn Davies CBE is former chairman of Standard Chartered PLC and former UK minister of state for trade, investment and small business.

John Davis is managing director of BCSG, a fast-growing firm offering cloud-based applications to small businesses.

Sir Charlie Mayfield is chairman of John Lewis Partnership and Chairman of the UK Commission for Employment and Skills (UK-CES).

Mariana Mazzucato is RM Phillips professor in the economics of innovation at Sussex University. She is the author of *The Entrepreneurial State: Debunking Private vs. Public Sector Myths*.

Jim O'Neill is an economist and former chairman of Goldman Sachs Asset Management.

Carlota Perez is Centennial Professor at the London School of Economics, Professor of Technology and Development, Nurkse Institute, Estonia and Honorary Professor, SPRU, University of Sussex. She is the author of *Technological Revolutions and Financial Capital: The Dynamics of Bubbles and Golden Ages*.

Roy Rickhuss is general secretary of Community Union.

Sir Peter Rigby is an entrepreneur, chairman and chief executive of Rigby Group PLC. He was chair of Coventry and Warwickshire Local Enterprise Partnership (CWLEP).

Lord David Sainsbury is a former UK minister of science and innovation and chancellor of the University of Cambridge.

Matthew Taylor is chief executive of the Royal Society for the encouragement of Arts, Manufactures and Commerce (RSA).

Chuka Umunna is UK Shadow Business Secretary and Member of Parliament for Streatham.

INTRODUCTION

How Britain Can Harness the Winds of Change

Chuka Umunna

One of the most important conversations I have had since being appointed by Ed Miliband as Shadow Business Secretary was with the late Nigel Doughty. Nigel was a successful entrepreneur, a life-long Labour supporter, fan—and former Chairman—of Nottingham Forest Football Club. He led the Party's Small Business Taskforce until his untimely death in 2012.

Shortly before he died, I was traveling with Nigel in Germany on a trip to learn lessons from business and political leaders there. I think we were in Frankfurt when we were discussing what we had seen, and its relevance to the challenges before Britain in the 21st century. Nigel explained to me his worries about the possible negative effects of the incoming technological tide and the "destruction" that it was—and is—exacting at the same time as creating tremendous new opportunities. Our job as progressives, he argued, was to work out how to harness that change to benefit everyone, not just a small internationally mobile elite. We both deeply believed that Government had an active role to play in empowering people to meet their aspirations and dreams in a changed world. It was why I went into politics.

Every day in my South London constituency I get glimpses of what Nigel was talking about. The economic and technological changes convulsing our world are exciting and can bring enormous benefits. But they can have starkly negative aspects too. I am always delighted to see new businesses opening, new trading links being forged, people having more control over their lives. But on the other side of the ledger, I witness the steadily growing gulf between those who are connected to this new world—who have the skills and support to make the most of it—and those who do not, left stranded as others run ahead.

Nigel may no longer be with us, but the spirit of his argument lives on. It survives in the final report of the Small Business Taskforce, which continues to influence Labour's vision for a nation both enterprising and inclusive. And it survives as a "how to" guide to the task of making Britain ready for the challenges it faces: thinking long term; being optimistic but vigilant; being ready to learn from others; and, most of all, always striving through our common endeavour to improve outcomes for the many, not just the few.

THE PERENNIAL GALE

Nigel used the word "destruction," and increasingly others have referred to "creative destruction," to neatly encapsulate the task before us. The latter was coined by Joseph Schumpeter, an Austrian-American economist, as a description of the constructive churn of a market economy. He talked of constant innovation and technological change as a "perennial gale" battering individuals and businesses. In his scheme, those who can channel this blustery change, windmill-like, survive (and sometimes thrive). Those who cannot get blown away.

Today we are seeing winds of change blowing through towns and communities up and down Britain. They have gusted even more harshly in the past few years with the rise of new global economic powers in the East and the emergence of new labour-saving technology. In some places, people have had the tools to harness what these winds of change can bring. Think of London with its global reach, Cambridge with its IT and biotechnology firms, Leeds and Edinburgh with their financial services. Some—but by no means all—of the people in those cities and elsewhere are thriving in this world of Bitcoin, Kickstarter and AirBnB.

But millions of others have no such luck. The wages of ordinary workers have become disconnected from growth in the economy overall. Ed Miliband has defined the task of remaking this link as the challenge of our age. Our task is to build a high wage, high skill economy, with good jobs offering a career and a future. Many have drawn attention to the steady hollowing out of our labour market. Lots of jobs are being created at the top, among bankers, lawyers and consultants. Lots of jobs are being created at the bottom, among cleaners, carers and administrative staff. We should celebrate the creation of these jobs. But we should also regret the decline of the in-betweeners: those in well-paid, secure jobs in the middle which require technical skills. Like a gale, it can throw things we thought had deep roots and foundations up in the air.

This decline matters. It means the steady exclusion of people from the benefits of the globalised, high-tech economy. In the past, many factory workers and middle managers could make enough money to buy a home, sustain a family, own a car and enjoy an annual holiday. Increasingly, that is not the case.

All over the world, governments are confronting a similar phenomenon. The places that are seeing the greatest success (Singapore, Stuttgart, San Francisco, Scandinavia, Shanghai and Sydney—to name just some of the "s" entries) are doing so by enabling more and more people to build the windmill that is needed: strengthening social resilience and the collective ability to absorb risk; reforming vocational education; increasing access to finance for new ventures; and guiding entrepreneurs into new markets.

Britain can learn huge amounts from such places. But it has a distinctive economy of its own. We need to adapt such lessons to our own situation.

THE BOOK YOU ARE ABOUT TO READ

It is in this spirit that I have edited this collection. The goal is to stimulate debate about how Britain can "own the future"—how, with energy and optimism, we can harness the changes ahead and make them work for us all. Naturally, we will only be able to succeed in the modern world by learning from those of different backgrounds and experiences, and by being open to new ideas and thinking from any source. So the chapters that follow are the work of 14 contributors from business, government and academia, and from different parts of the globe.

The focus of the book and its structure date from a speech I made at the EEF's Annual Dinner in March this year about how Britain could make it in a rapidly changing world. There I argued that it would only be through aligning the policy horizons of politicians with the investment horizons of our businesses that we could build an economy generating balanced, sustainable and inclusive growth. Reflecting this focus on the longer term, I called Labour's plan to earn and grow our way to a higher standard of living for all "Agenda 2030."

That evening, I sketched the outlines of this approach, built on a foundation of fiscal responsibility. To succeed would take more than business as usual on the upswing of a long-delayed recovery. It would require real reform of our economy—not big spending— sustained over a long period of time. It is why Labour has set out plans to liberate the talents of all of our people, investing in everyone and creating the platforms from which they can succeed— through skilled jobs and careers or through enterprise, and in every corner of our nation. Extending opportunity in this way has always been Labour's defining political goal. Today it is an economic imperative.

It is why we must win shares of new markets by remaining at the cutting edge of innovation, solving tomorrow's problems today. It is why we have set out plans for a challenging but stable partnership between government and business, with well-functioning markets, an industrial strategy focused on long-term value creation and long-term infrastructure planning and decision making. And, in a rapidly changing global context, it requires Britain to remain resolutely outward focused and positively engaged with the world beyond our shores. It is why Labour would reform the EU to make it more growth focused, not head for the exit—because of its value to us as both our nearest and largest market and a gateway to emerging markets beyond.

Here this broad approach provides the structure for the contributions in this book—the changing global context, the challenge of inclusive growth, the innovation imperative and a long-term partnership between business and government. Each are addressed by entrepreneurs and economists, trade union and business leaders, thinkers and doers. They each accepted the challenge to write on these themes, build on the ideas and take them in new directions.

As a result, the pieces making up this book are not the work of a single mind. They are diverse and, in some places, discordant. Throughout my travels, meetings and visits, I have always valued the input of people with their own unique perspective on the big questions. Only by listening, consulting, asking questions and being collegiate about our challenges can we hope to solve them.

While being true to our values, the biggest mistake we could make as politicians would be to limit the pool of ideas from which we draw because of tribal instincts or party lines. If we want to find answers that improve life for all in Britain, I believe strongly that we must actively encourage debate and seek out ideas from different perspectives. So this volume is designed to trigger and enrich debates, not bring them to a definitive close. Equally importantly, I want to stress that these contributions do not amount to an endorsement of Labour by the authors, or of the authors by Labour. Each writes here in a purely independent capacity and in the spirit of a free exchange of ideas.

I want to put on record my gratitude to all of those who have contributed. They are an extremely accomplished group whose records speak for themselves, and whose advice and insights are sought after across the globe. It is a great honour to be able to present their views on the path Britain should embark on in the coming years. I am grateful to them for the time and care they have taken to contribute, and for their ideas they present here.

INSTITUTIONS, PRODUCTIVITY AND CONNECTIONS

No summary can capture the full depth and insight of the chapters that follow. However, three themes that run through them should, in particular, be brought to the reader's attention.

The first of these is the need to increase Britain's productivity rate, which is unimpressive by international comparison. Contributors from Jim O'Neill to Roy Rickhuss and Sir Charlie Mayfield all point to the critical importance of raising productivity if we are to maintain and improve living standards. Productivity is a function of investment—in skills and human capital. As Lord Sainsbury puts it, "Instead of deploying a fixed pool of factors of production, firms and nations seek to improve the quality of factors, raise the productivity with which they are utilised and create new ones."

But how to do so? Lord Sainsbury points to the need for policy makers to become much more attentive to the internal operations of firms: how they might accumulate the organisational and technological capabilities that enable them to outcompete others. This must include, as Roy Rickhuss argues, how UK firms might close the current gap on employee engagement and participation compared with our competitors. Matthew Taylor asks how we might realise the promise of "mass creativity" to enable people to lead more fulfilling—as well as more productive—lives, and he considers the organisational enablers and barriers. Contributors ranging from Sherry Coutu to David Cleevely make powerful arguments for the need to focus support on helping firms to scale up and grow to their full potential, a challenge that is brought to life by the experiences of John Davis in growing tech firm BCSG, as well as Billy Boyle, co-founder of Owlstone Nanotech. Many point to the importance of clusters in supporting business success, just part of the wider institutional framework needed to drive productivity growth.

This focus on institutions and institutional innovation is the second ongoing theme. Carlota Perez's bold vision of the future will require concerted leadership from politicians at an international as well as national level to set the direction for technology enabled, global, green growth. At the UK level, Ha-Joon Chang and Antonio Andreoni argue that industrial policy needs to come home—embraced fully as a part of our national history as well as our future. They point to the need for stronger institutional linkages across and between sectoral approaches, a need to shift the focus to the long term and a need for a serious upgrade in our technological infrastructure.

Indeed, the critical priority that must be given to developing our national system of innovation is also emphasised by Lord Sainsbury. Mariana Mazzucato further reinforces this argument; it is enhanced by her analysis of the state's dynamic role in past innovations. It is, she argues, only by correctly understanding the role that each actor—including the state—plays in a healthy system of innovation that we can foster "inclusive" as well as "smart" growth in the future. Finally, Sir Peter Rigby emphasises the spatial dimension of institutional innovation that is needed. He draws on his own experience of chairing a Local Enterprise Partnership to make the case for why LEPs need to move from success "against the odds" to being given the power and resources needed to drive growth in regional economies.

The third ongoing theme is that of Britain as a global hub. Lord Davies talks about trade long having been "the lifeblood" of the UK economy. Jim O'Neill notes how this history, our culture and other unique endowments shape our future opportunities:

> I have often described London as the "BRIC capital of the world" in recent years. I occasionally wonder whether this is an early sign of what could happen to the UK if it succeeds more broadly as a trading nation, offering more affluent consumers in the emerging world the sophisticated, higher-value products they desire. Our time zone and our use of the English language give us an edge that virtually no other country has. If we can maintain

high-quality finance and legal systems, Brand UK is well placed
to prosper in the world I envisage.

None of the above is assured. Britain is a medium-sized country
on the fringes of an old and historic continent. We need to earn our
place in the new world economy. We need to co-opt the big changes
that are taking place around us. As Lord Davies points out, "If we
stand still as a nation, we will fall behind. To thrive in this future,
we must be prepared." To him, this means clearer long-term direction, closer partnership between business and government and
stronger links abroad, as well as better support for small and medium-sized exporters.

Britain has faced such tumultuous challenges before and is
uniquely well endowed to meet them today: we have many of the
world's greatest seats of learning, one of its most dynamic services
industries and unrivalled international connections through the EU,
the Commonwealth, the "special relationship" and our well-inte-
grated diaspora communities. We possess what may be the world's
premium metropolis—and at least a dozen other cities that are rapidly gaining the confidence, specialism and powers to compete on
the international stage. Britain has an excellent future.

In bringing this publication together, I owe a real debt to Michael
McTernan and his colleagues at Policy Network—in particular,
Claudia Chwalisz and Renaud Thillaye—for all their work. In addition, it would not have been possible without the support of Lord
Bhattacharyya and WMG. I would also like to thank Charlotte Bal-
nave, Jeremy Cliffe, Anna Coffey, Lisa Eynon, David Hale, Gabriel
Huntley, Jeff Masters and Jake Sumner. I am grateful to so many
other people who have inspired my thinking and contributed to my
ideas—from business and academia as well as politics, from within
the Labour family and well beyond it. This is a long list, and it
would be invidious to name some without naming all.

I want to say a particular thank you to all the businesses I have
had the privilege of visiting in the course of my work and the inspiration I have drawn from those who have started them, run them, or
work in them to create success. Last but not least, I must thank my

employers—the people of my constituency in Streatham—for granting me the privilege of representing you. What this book shows is that the world to come is full of opportunity. Our challenge is to ensure that every person in Streatham—and throughout the country—can take advantage of these opportunities and fulfil their aspirations.

This book is dedicated to Nigel Doughty and to all those—in the private and public sectors, from the shop floor to the boardroom—in whose creativity, energies and skill our nation's future lies.

London, July 28, 2014

I

The Changing Global Context

BRITAIN AND THE WORLD IN 2030

Jim O'Neill

Tapping into the BRIC and MINT countries is vital for inclusive prosperity. The challenge is to succeed as a trading nation, offering more affluent consumers in the emerging world the sophisticated, higher-value products they will increasingly desire. Brand UK is well placed to prosper.

I have spent more than 30 years in business and economic forecasting. If this time has taught me anything, it is this: no matter how strong your views of the future, you can't let one of them dominate your planning for the possible outcomes. So when it comes to Britain's planning for the world in 2030, it is important to remain adaptable and not to put all your eggs in one basket. While it is right to have a clear view about where our strengths lie, it is dangerous to be too prescriptive. In recent years, various policymakers have declared export targets for particular sectors, often with the notion of doubling them by the end of 2020. While such an aspiration is understandable and admirable, the reality is that the biggest driver of any country's exports is demand in the key markets. And clearly these conditions are not easily influenced.

THE RISE OF THE BRIC AND MINT COUNTRIES

Having made this comment on the uncertainties of the future, I do of course have quite a clear view of what the world might look like in 2030. It is one where China has reached the same size as the US economy (in US$ nominal terms), where India is on the verge of becoming one of the five largest economies in the world and where the remaining BRIC nations of Brazil and Russia—together with the MINT countries of Mexico, Indonesia, Nigeria and Turkey—are all striving to be in the top 10 economies.

After the Great Recession of 2008–2009, many people assumed that these large emerging economies would continue to see their presence in the world economy rise, mainly thanks to the probable slow recovery of the so-called developed world. Today, such optimism in the emerging world is not so widespread. Concerns about their economies' prospects have grown, against a backdrop of increased confidence in the US economy, improving hopes for Japan and tentative hopes that the worst fears for continental Europe will not materialise.

Although it is unlikely that every major economy in the world can grow strongly at the same time, that does not mean that ongoing economic growth in the emerging world will hinder growth within developed countries. In this regard, a key issue for any trade-oriented country is its relative contribution to world growth. It is not commonly known, for example, that world GDP growth in the decade 2001–2010 averaged 3.7%, despite the Great Recession and the earlier bursting of the global IT bubble in 2000–2001, both in the same decade. This growth was higher than in the two previous decades 1981–1990 and 1991–2000, in which it averaged around 3.3%, and was preceded by weaker growth in the 1970s. This was mainly explained by the rise of China (and, to a lesser degree, that of the other BRIC and large emerging economies) and despite the challenges facing many Western economies.

Since 2011, I have assumed that for the current decade, world GDP growth will average an even stronger 4.1%. This is based on the continued rise of the BRIC and MINT economies, and the absence of crises on the scale of 2000–2001 and 2008–2009. More-over, this assumption is predicated on an expectation that China will grow by less, specifically by around 7.5%. With it, the growth rate of the BRIC countries will be softer than in the last decade, even though their contribution will rise. At the end of 2013, China's economy was around US$9.2 trillion in size, bigger than the combined size of the German, French and Italian economies, and about half the size of the American one. From a global GDP perspective, China growing by 7.5% in 2014 is broadly equivalent to the US growing by 4%. So although China is "slowing," it is contributing more to the world economy.

THE CHANGING CHINESE AND AMERICAN ECONOMIES

For the two decades up to 2030, my best guess is that China will grow by around 6.5%. This should be sufficient to take it towards $30 trillion in current 2013 US$, slightly bigger than the US. Crucially, this growth is likely to be different from the growth China has seen for most of the 1990–2010 period, fuelled less by exports and state investment and more by domestic consumption. For the rest of the world, providing what more affluent Chinese consumers want will become an increasingly important part of international business. So the winners and losers of this "new" China may well be different from the winners and losers of the old China. As I will discuss below, the UK could well be one of the winners, reaping the rewards of a China that is increasingly interested in value-added services and better-quality products rather than commodity-intensive and basic goods.

As China changes, so, too, does the US. We are already seeing signs of the US emerging as a somewhat different economy to that of before the Great Recession. The country will cease to be the world's number one importer, especially of energy but also of other consumer products. Consequently, its companies will join the competitive battle to export to China and other rising emerging nations.

In my judgement, the US will be able to grow at a rate in the vicinity of 2.0–2.5% between now and 2030.

On one simple model, what happens to the US and China will be the key driving force for the rest of the world. They will easily remain the dominant economies, accounting for at least a third of the global economy, with no other economy coming close to half their individual sizes. In such a simplified model, it is important to think of the US and China as gradually moving towards different sorts of economies to those familiar to many. The US becoming a bit more like the old China—saving more and consuming less, with a smaller current account deficit. China becoming a bit more like the old US—saving less and consuming more, with a smaller current account surplus.

Critical to the success of China and the US, and fundamental to the world as a whole, is the way in which the two countries handle relations with one another, as well as with everyone else. This transcends global peace and security, as well as international monetary and economic policy matters. One would imagine that the monetary system will gradually become less dependent on the US$ and that the role of the RMB will rise. In this context, the UK and its international financial role from London should be well placed to benefit. Policymakers should certainly be prepared for this.

OTHER MAJOR ECONOMIES

As for the other emerging economies, India has the best chance of becoming a global economic power. Due to historical ties and language, this could be particularly beneficial to the UK. At the time of writing, China's economy is one-and-a-half times the size of the Brazilian, Indian and Russian economies combined, each of which is around US$2 trillion depending on their exchange rates. Yet, with its powerful demographics and scope for huge improvements in urbanisation, governance and productivity, India has a reasonable chance of achieving stronger GDP growth rates than China between now and 2030. The incoming Modi government has been given a platform by the electorate to force through much-required structural change and I think there are some grounds for excitement here. India has a reasonable chance of rediscovering economic growth of 7–8%, however the potential for even stronger growth should not be ruled out.

For Brazil and Russia, unless they can reduce their dependency on commodities and government spending, they might not return to the growth rates enjoyed in the last decade. Economic growth in the 2–3% vicinity, rather than 5–6%, could well become a reality. As disappointing as these rates may be, they will likely be higher than those of Japan and continental Europe (given the poor demographics of these latter countries), and it is probable that their share of global GDP will continue to rise modestly.

Several other emerging economies, including most of the MINT countries and some parts of Africa, could continue to experience very strong (and potentially faster) growth rates, comparable to those of China and India.

By 2030, the world's top 10 economies will come in a very different order. China will in all likelihood hold the number one spot, closely followed by the US. Japan and Germany are expected to stay in the top 10, whilst France and Italy could well slip down the rankings and will be fighting harder than ever to remain part of this elite. The UK has a chance of remaining in the top 10—given our favourable demographics—but only if we can improve our productivity and remain adaptable. In addition to Brazil, India will almost definitely be included, and both are expected to see their ranks in the top 10 rise. Russia will be vying for a place in the top group, alongside Indonesia and Mexico.

UK AND GLOBAL TRADE PATTERNS

In recent years, the UK has remained absorbed by its historical trade relationships with the US, while its position in the EU has become more fraught. I think it is quite plausible that relationships with Europe in general will become more difficult, not least because the

EU will continue to see its share of the world economy and trade decline. While most of today's generation of British leaders see their prime relationships as being those with the EU and its largest economies, this is likely to change. For example, China might replace France as Germany's number one export market. And for other strong European exporting nations, shifts in the same direction—if not the same magnitude—are likely. This will probably mean that the economic ties that bring so many continental economies together will be loosened, although the political and security ties should remain just as strong. How the EU adjusts in terms of its overall structure is difficult to predict, and while it remains important for the UK to have good relations with Europe, the strength of our relationships with China, India and the rising emerging world will become increasingly significant.

I have often described London as the "BRIC capital of the world" in recent years. I occasionally wonder whether this is an early sign of what could happen to the UK if it succeeds more broadly as a trading nation, offering more affluent consumers in the emerging world the sophisticated, higher-value products they desire. Our time zone and our use of the English language give us an edge that virtually no other country has. If we can maintain high-quality finance and legal systems, Brand UK is well placed to prosper in the world I envisage.

At the start of this coalition government, our Chancellor made reference to the fact that we exported more to Ireland than the BRIC countries combined, in an attempt to justify our role in the Euro crisis bailout. Fortunately, this is no longer the case—but there is more to do. By 2030, we will probably be more concerned about a major crisis in the BRIC and MINT world than in the Euro zone. Whether we are will be the test of whether the UK economy has adjusted appropriately. If so, we will be doing rather well.

Jim O'Neill is an economist and former chairman of Goldman Sachs Asset Management.

A NEW AGE OF TECHNOLOGICAL PROGRESS

Carlota Perez

To seize the opportunity of our great surge of technological development, we need a national and global consensus between business, government and society that will do for the 21st century what social democracy did for the 20th.

The world appears to be changing at an unprecedented pace. Information technology is displacing or reshaping industry after industry; rapid globalisation is leading to power shifts between nations, and the threat of global warming is becoming ever more present.

In fact, we have been here before. A deeper understanding of both history and technology can help us respond to these challenges and find a prosperous path ahead. What we can see is that there is nothing inevitable about how these forces will reshape our world. This will be dependent not on the technological, global and environmental forces, but on the socio-political choices we make to take best advantage of them.

FIVE TECHNOLOGICAL REVOLUTIONS

Technological advance might appear as a continuous process, but in fact the world has gone through five technological upheavals since the Industrial Revolution in the late 1770s.[1] Each of these shifts (see figure 2.1) brought with it a whole set of powerful new industries and infrastructures—canals, railways, electricity, highways, telecoms and the internet—which have enabled a quantum leap in productivity and quality in all industries. These technological leaps have also widened and deepened market spaces, shifted the centres of industrial dynamism and changed the rankings in world power.

The Industrial Revolution introduced mechanisation, changing the role of skills in production, and initiated the era of British power. The following railway age led to the rise of the educated and entrepreneurial middle classes. The third, from the end of the 19th century, was the first globalisation based on empires and saw the emergence of Germany and the US as challengers of British hegemony. Subsequently, the US led the age of the automobile and mass production, bringing the American way of life to the working classes and increasing the role of the State in economic stability. The current information and telecommunications technology (ICT) revolution has enabled the second globalisation; yet its full transformative impact on society is still to be defined.

As Schumpeter rightly noted—echoing Marx—capitalism is "incessantly revolutionising the economic structure from within, incessantly destroying the old one, incessantly creating the new one."[2] However, in each case, after two or three decades of frenzied experimentation with the new technologies and a bubble collapse or two, society has had to learn to facilitate and guide the unleashing of these new forces in order to increase the social benefits that can be gained from their stable deployment.

TWO DIFFERENT PERIODS

Each of these revolutions has driven a *great surge of development* that takes half a century or more to spread unevenly across the economy. Each occurs in two distinct periods—installation and deployment—with a transitional phase in the middle that is marked by a major bubble collapse and recession. Figure 2.1 shows the historical sequence of the great surges with their equivalent periods in parallel.

It is important to note the difference between the "gilded" nature of the prosperities that characterise the initial decades of each great surge and that of the golden ages that follow after the bubble collapses and the subsequent recessions. The installation period is one of extravagant "Great Gatsby" prosperity that sets up the new infrastructures and spreads a new common sense practice across the business world and across society. It is finance that leads the investment process, backing the new entrepreneurs, spreading new technologies and forcing the old to modernise. This period also results

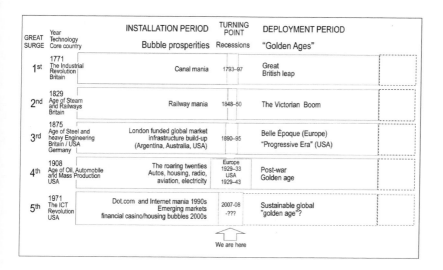

Figure 2.1. Five Great Surges: Bubbles, Recessions and "Golden Ages"

in an increasing polarisation of income through differential asset inflation, financial manipulation and major shifts in the location of jobs and in the types and levels of skills required.

The prosperities of the deployment period of each surge, by contrast, are seen as "golden ages" because they tend to reverse some of the destruction and polarisation resulting from installation. It is in these later periods that the potential of the revolution enables innovation, investment, jobs and expansion across the economy. These are the times when synergy is attained between the new industries, the modernised old industries and complementary activities that complete the new fabric of the economy and create the new jobs that counteract those displaced by technical change.

The fabric of the economy is neither pre-determined nor defined by technology. It is a socio-political choice, and one that arises out of the collapse of the bubble (or bubbles) that end the period of installation. This collapse reveals the inequalities that arose in that period, along with the decoupling of the speculative financial casino from the production economy. The recession that follows results from the structural changes brought about by the revolution. As the 1930s showed, this cannot be reversed by markets alone. Reviving the flagging economy and going back to business as usual is impossible because economic growth post-bubble requires a fundamental redirection. In these transitional periods, leaders need to recognise the irreversible changes and to design a socio-institutional framework that achieves a good match with the specific new potential installed.

THE SHAPING OF THE POST-WWII BOOM

The post-War mass production revolution is the most recent example of a full cycle of installation and deployment. The potential of those technologies was shaped very differently by the Western democracies, Hitler and Stalin. In the West, the power of mass production and the infrastructure enabled by the automobile was turned into a consumer-led process of continuous innovation, investment and expansion. Yet in the middle of the depression it was difficult to recognise the vast range of viable innovations connected with plastics, energy intensive materials, energy using devices and the new mass production methods, capable of creating a consumerist way of life that could fuel economic expansion for decades. At the time, assembly line manufacturing and the mechanisation of agriculture had generated the same fears of "secular stagnation"[3] that today arise from globalisation, ICT and robotics.

The revival success resulted from a synergistic combination of institutional innovations such as the credit system, labour union-secured salaries, unemployment and mortgage insurance, free or subsidised education and healthcare, and a progressive tax structure. The state funded many of these institutional innovations as well as the Cold War, the other direction of innovation mostly funded by the state. It was a positive-sum game established between business and society that led to the greatest boom ever seen, aided by international innovations that included the World Bank, the International Monetary Fund, the dollar being used as "gold standard," the General Agreement on Tariffs and Trade, and the United Nations.

We are now in an equivalent moment in history, requiring similarly bold thinking and measures. The levels of unemployment and inequality brought about by globalisation and ICT technologies, along with the increasing environmental challenges resulting from the previous technological revolution, threaten social cohesion and security. The installation period of the current revolution established the worldwide web, enabling planetary financial markets and the organisation of industry in global value networks. Yet the capacity of information technologies to transform every single industry and activity, and to spawn innovations across the board, has only barely been applied. The current growth and innovation potential in industry after industry, in old and complementary activities is huge, but its profitability is too uncertain to attract massive finance. Unleashing that potential in a coherent direction could lead to a sustainable global golden age that would do for developing economies what the post-war boom did for advanced countries of the West. What is lacking is a set of policies to tilt the playing field in a clear direction in order to generate synergies—suppliers, distribution, skills and other shared factors—as occurred with suburbanisation in the post-war boom. At present, most of the many diverse and disparate innovations that are technologically possible are seen as uncertain in terms of markets and profitability. It is the combination of dynamic demand and convergent direction that will provide the conditions for innovation and investment to thrive, bringing a global economic revival.

"GREEN GROWTH" AS THE NEW DIRECTION FOR INNOVATION

The most promising direction for a global boom is "green growth."[4] In my understanding, this does *not* mean simply applying renewable energies to the economy and the social institutions of the oil age. Rather, "green" is a direction for deployment in which, as suggested at the start of this chapter, technology, globalisation and the environmental challenges turn from obstacles to solutions for the current problems related to growth, jobs and competitiveness. Green growth would act as a selection mechanism to guide the trajectories of innovation in a convergent direction that creates externalities common to all. In the process, it would involve a complete redefinition of "the good life."

What does this mean? Historically, every technological revolution has led to a radical change in consumption patterns consistent with the range of products shaped by the new technologies: from Victorian living in the mid-19th century to the cosmopolitan style of the Belle Époque and to the American way of life. If what motivates the new billions of middle-income consumers in the emerging world is aspiring to the same suburbanised, disposable living that drove the mass production boom in the 20th century, they—and their Western counterparts—will soon stumble against resource scarcity and unaffordable prices. Instead, the technologies enabled by ICT provide a wide range of possibilities for changing the proportion of tangible and intangible goods and services in the patterns of both consumption and production. This could enable a vast increase in the productivity of resources at the same time as a significant reduction in energy and materials consumption through the redesign of products and the optimisation of logistics.[5]

The growing use of renting and collaboration is already lengthening the life of products and encouraging a multi-user model of distribution, diminishing the amount of materials and energy required to satisfy individual consumption needs. Smart electric grids are beginning to allow the interactive production and consumption of energy and could do much more. Experiments in the "circular economy" are yielding impressive business results. Nano-materials and other advances are promising leaps in quality and durability of products. The long predicted reduction of paper consumption might finally begin to happen, through e-books, tablets, internet information and other intangible means of communication. Alongside the ever more versatile ICT devices, local organic food, sustainable design, electric cars, bicycles and healthy living form the new aspirational lifestyles, replacing consumerism, passivity, obesity and disposability.

THE SHAPE OF THE FUTURE

Today, the prevailing conventional wisdom, based on recent experience, is a poor source of inspiration. The new weak trends, especially those led by the young "digital natives," are the shape of the future. At times of unused technological potential, it is safer to be bold than to be restrained by "realism."

At present, the jobless rates in many advanced countries are unacceptable and the current policies are, at best, only bringing anaemic and unstable growth. A courageous policy of funding green growth research and procurement,[6] plus strong measures stimulating innovation and investment in the revamping of the built environment and a redesign of products, services, distribution and maintenance systems along green lines, would radically reduce the jobless rate in each country. Imagine regulation clearly favouring true durability of electrical appliances, for instance, by requiring the manufacturer to take responsibility for disposal—as the EU's Waste Electrical and Electronic Equipment Directive[7] partly does. This is likely to spawn at least three innovative high employment processes: a rental and maintenance service, a disassembly industry favouring component and material reuse and the redesign of all products for ease of maintenance, recycling and upgrading. All those activities are already growing at a slow pace in industries large and small and in different countries at different rhythms. The circular economy,[8] industrial symbiosis (in which one industry uses the other's by-products), cradle-to-cradle[9] and other experiments are spreading among pioneering companies that recognise the trends of the future. The shift from ownership to rental is already visible in the so-called "sharing economy"; it is easy to imagine it evolving with an Amazon-like used-products, web-based system and with chips identifying products and recording their use history.

As for producers, they may soon realise that they no longer need the "planned obsolescence" strategy. With the continuous entry of millions of new middle-income consumers across the world, they are more likely to confront resource price hikes than market saturation. Besides, what a rental model can do is to transform the high-quality luxury upper end of the market into the entry point. The richest will want the latest models, with all technological advances and design features, but from there on, each model would move to second-hand use, third-hand and so on, until those entering the consumption ladder can access it at very low cost.

We need to look at the trends initiated by the young and the pioneers, in the advanced and emerging countries, and imagine how to create the conditions that will accelerate such changes so they reach the tipping point and become a strong, transformative social and economic force. We need policies that tilt the playing field, making economically profitable what is technologically possible and can be socially beneficial.

THINK GLOBAL; ACT NATIONAL AND LOCAL

Green growth can also lead to a global re-specialisation—with enough markets for all to grow, while addressing the increasing risks of food, water and raw material scarcities and climate change. If the process of full global development intensifies, demand for goods, equipment, engineering and infrastructure would be enough to mobilise the—also growing—economies of Asia, as well as those of the advanced world. In turn, the rising demand for materials and food would provide dynamic markets for natural resource producers at increasing prices. This would allow them to fund their own development, closing the feedback loop of demand for capital goods from the more advanced countries.

Of course, that complex process of interactive global market growth is only realistic if it is environmentally sustainable. It will need to use more expensive and specialised materials, in order to require less quantity per product and to allow for greater durability. It will mean more infrastructure and equipment, but adapted to the climatic conditions using low or no-carbon renewable energy and energy storage. This green direction, in turn, would widen the market for that sort of equipment, reducing costs and expanding markets even further.

The same holds for consumption patterns. The focus would shift from the old consumerism to healthy lives, with a high proportion of intangibles in consumption, including more communication and creativity, more exercise and community activities, more education—both face-to-face and computer-based—more caring and sharing activities and so on, as well as significantly greater durability and recyclability of all tangible products. The "good green life" has to be creative, healthy, pleasurable and comfortable. It cannot be based on guilt or on sacrifices. It has to be what people aspire to as they climb the income ladder and the ladder has to be functioning for all, both the new climbers and those that have slid down. All that will require the support of adequate and imaginative institutional innovations.

The green transformation would also involve the gradual redesign of cities and the improvement of rural quality of life, stimulating both wealth-creating and community activities, so that migration is no longer the best option. The shift would probably be as gradual as suburbanisation was in its time and would need as much support from governments, business and the media as was required then, demanding complex consensus processes and wide-ranging alliances.[10] Both processes would call forth investment and jobs.

This direction for innovation makes sense not only for environmental, social and economic reasons but also because it is consistent with the nature of the ICT paradigm. The old hierarchical pyramid with top-down control is obsolete. We see the concept of networks being applied all around us by new entrepreneurs, in the thousands of apps connecting through the smartphone platforms. We also see it in the way global corporations organise their value chains and power structures. Under the radar, there is the flourishing of the sharing and the collaborative economy, the open source movement and the many imaginative ways of using the internet for improving the quality of life. The eventual combination of these complementary ways of using the transformative power of ICT—including in the organisation of government—may define the quality of life and the quantity of jobs.

THE TASK FOR LEADERS TODAY

Today it is not possible to bring stable long-term growth in the context of an isolated national economy. The ICT revolution has already created the conditions for the globalisation of the economy, such that national policies are now mostly defined as choices within the global space. Those choices would be more likely to bring a global sustainable golden age if they are coherent and mutually reinforcing across countries. And within each country, the quality of life of citizens must be prioritised over the no longer national interests of the financial world.[11]

Thus, the question today should not be: Can we afford the welfare state with less money? In that case, the solution can only be austerity and giving up on a fair society. The adequate question, from the perspective of history and innovation, is this: How can we use the new technological potential to put the economy on a growth path towards full employment and increasing well-being? That is the question that will call forth the required imagination towards technological, social, organisational and policy innovation.

It is time to create a national and global consensus between business, government and society that will do for the 21st century what social democracy did for the 20th. The legitimacy of capitalism rests on fulfilling its promise of achieving the common good through individual pursuit of wealth and power. Installation periods, and especially bubbles, bring the system to extreme individualism and to insensitivity to the plight of non-winners and the impoverished; bubble collapses and the ensuing deployment periods tend to rein this in and put a stronger focus on the common good. Conditions are now set for a global synergistic and sustainable growth process. But achieving it successfully requires the right socio-political choices. That is the challenge for leaders in this generation.

Carlota Perez is Centennial Professor at the London School of Economics, Professor of Technology and Development, Nurkse Institute, Estonia and Honorary Professor, SPRU, University of Sussex. She is the author of *Technological Revolutions and Financial Capital: the Dynamics of Bubbles and Golden Ages*.

NOTES

1. See Schumpeter, J.A. (1939:1982) *Business Cycles*. Philadelphia: Porcupine Press; Freeman, C., and Perez, C. (1988) "Structural Crises of Adjustment: Business Cycles and Investment Behaviour" in Dosi et al. (eds.), *Technical Change and Economic Theory*. London, Pinter. pp. 38–66; and Perez, C. (2002) *Technological Revolutions and Financial*

Capital: The Dynamics of Bubbles and Golden Ages. Cheltenham: Edward Elgar.

2.   Schumpeter, J.A. (1942:1987) *Capitalism, Socialism and Democracy*. London: Unwin. p. 83.

3.   The term was used recently by L. Summers in "Why stagnation might prove to be the new normal," *Financial Times*, December 15, 2013, available from http://www.ft.com/cms/s/2/87cb15ea-5d1a-11e3-a55800144feabdc0.html#axzz35Bf2xOBb (accessed 22.04.14). This term is also part of the argument of the techno-pessimists such as Gordon, R. (2012) "Is U.S Economic Growth Over? Faltering Innovation Confronts The Six Headwinds," Working Paper 18315, National Bureau of Economic Research, August 2012. http://www.nber.org/papers/wI8315.

4.   For a thorough discussion of the various meanings attributed to the term, see Jacobs, M. (2012) "Green Growth: Economic Theory and Political Discourse." Working Paper No. 108, Centre for Climate change and Policy, October. Available at http://www.lse.ac.uk/GranthamInstitute/wp-content/uploads/2012/10/WP92-green-growth-economic-theory-political-discourse.pdf (accessed 16/07/2014).

5.   If energy and materials prices continue to vary at a much higher level than in the 20th century, it could become more profitable to innovate for increasing resource productivity than for increasing labour productivity.

6.   See Mazzucato, M. (2013a) *The Entrepreneurial State: Debunking private vs. public sector myths*. London: Anthem Press (discussing the need for an entrepreneurial state).

7.   European Union (2012) Directive 2012/19/EU of the European Parliament and of the Council of 4 July 2012 on waste electrical and electronic equipment (WEEE), in the Official Journal of the European Union, L 197, 24 July 2012. Available from http://eur-lex.europa.eu/legal-content/EN/TXT/?uri=OJ:L:2012:197:TOC (accessed 11.04.14).

8.   Ellen MacArthur Foundation (2012/2013) Towards the circular economy: Economic and business rationale for an accelerated transition, *Circular Economy Report* Vol. 1&2.

9.   Braungart, M., and McDonough, W. (2009) *Cradle to Cradle. Remaking the Way We Make Things*. New York: Northpoint Press.

10.   For interesting discussions on the political issues of the green transformation, see Lockwood, M. (2014) "The political dynamics of green transformations." EPG Working Paper No. 1403, University of Exeter.

Available at http://projects.exeter.ac.uk/igov/wp-content/uploads/2014/04/ WP-8-The-political-dynamics-of-green-transformations.pdf (accessed 16/ 07/2014); and Schmitz, H., and Becker, B. (2013) "From Sustainable Development to the Green Transformation: A Rough Guide." Grey Literature, IDS. March 8.

11. The current national-populist tendencies (and the anger against finance) are understandable and echo the 1930s. The perception of personal decline always leads to searching for culprits. Only bold policies that overcome the decline of the majorities will defeat the political shift.

TRADING PLACES: PREPARING BRITAIN FOR GLOBAL OPPORTUNITY

Lord Mervyn Davies

Britain must adapt to be ready for success in the world of the future, setting clear long-term direction, maintaining a commitment to openness, and supporting the export success of smaller firms.

Trade has long been the lifeblood of the British economy. The UK's stronghold as a trading nation was hit hard by the financial crisis and as it struggles to get back on its feet, the need for radical economic reform has never been so great. The shifting balance of world economic power makes this need for change all the more urgent, as growth in emerging high-potential economies increasingly outpaces that of the developed nations. Britain must renew its role as a dynamic trading nation, but it cannot do this through business as usual. The UK's ability to adapt, to innovate and to remain agile in the face of accelerated change will decide how the nation fares as a trading force of the future.

THE GLOBAL LANDSCAPE IS CHANGING FAST

Trade corridors are transforming. It was during my time as Head of Standard Chartered's Asian business that I began to appreciate the enormous potential of the emerging world. But even a decade ago, who would have expected so much focus on China's relationship with Brazil and Africa? The opportunities presented by a growing middle class in the so-called BRICs, as well as Nigeria, Indonesia and Vietnam, amongst others, are vast. Large new multinationals are becoming superpowers. These are not US or European multinationals but rather those from Indonesia, Singapore, China and India. Countries and corporates have to adapt to a massive shift in weighting and the UK must place much greater focus on emerging markets.

I truly believe that Britain's economy has much to celebrate and its businesses a huge amount to be proud of. Through the years, we have succeeded in establishing and maintaining thriving, global industries. We must build on this, and broaden the base of our success. We are home to some of the greatest business minds in the world; creating global leaders who are now acting as mentors to a generation of new and enthusiastic British talent. We must open up the talent pool, so all with potential have the chance to lead British business forward. We will only be making full use of our Nation's potential when we are world leaders in workplace equality, giving everyone—regardless of gender, race, age or background—the same opportunity to succeed.

THE CONTEXT FOR BRITISH BUSINESS IS CHANGING TOO

Business models are changing, and a new workplace is emerging. The full impact of the internet and social media revolutions is now hitting business. Customers are demanding more—more transparency, more customization and more accountability. Legacy issues are no longer a valid excuse for poor customer experience. And by the same token, employees expect more from their employers.

As the world gets smaller and country boundaries become blurred, young people have a different relationship with work. They will live longer and will have to work longer, and without the same pension net their parents enjoyed. Adaptability will be the watchword. Gone are the days when you would choose your profession at the age of 21 and remain loyal to this one occupation, and often one company, through to retirement. Those entering the jobs market today expect to try out at least two or three different careers. This flexibility cuts both ways, with employers having to adapt to demands for better work-life balance and mid-career breaks becoming the rule rather than the exception. Couple that with the increasing voice of women in the workplace, and it's a period of real change for employers and employees alike.

MAKING THE MOST OF BRITAIN'S STRENGTHS IN THE WORLD OF THE FUTURE

In the context of change, both at home and abroad, Britain must adapt fast to succeed. First, as an ex-banker and ex–trade minister, I can appreciate more than most the central role that small firms play in creating jobs, distributing wealth and ensuring the UK remains competitive. We need more "role model" small and medium-sized firms to trade with tenacity and ambition—a British Mittelstand, if you like. We need real focus on making exporting even easier, with Export Credits Guarantees and other finance that really works to boost trade. We need more collaboration and stronger partnership between the trade associations, Chambers of Commerce and other major trade bodies—following the example of Germany and France, which are far more progressive in their integration.

Second, Britain retains an important and influential banking industry, despite recent problems. To ensure that we maintain this stronghold, we should be encouraging greater innovation and product development from our banks. Trade is increasingly moving away from Letter of Credit towards a system that favours Open Account. So banks in the UK and elsewhere, operating in the context of Basle 3, must realise that trade is the lifeblood of our future. However, it is not just banks—Government and regulators must also wake up to the strategic importance of trade and act upon it. Do we need a new charter on trade? Do we need to recognise and celebrate our export success more? Do we need greater social media coverage on international business? The answer is a resounding yes, so let's get on with it.

Third, like corporations, countries need long-term plans that are above the immediate demands of day-to-day politics and petty snipping. We need a genuine focus on the long term, based on an improved dialogue between business and government on what business needs to thrive. Constant chopping and changing of direction raises the risks of investing—and with it the cost—while a longer-term approach will give firms the clarity and certainty they need to make needed investments for the future. Ensuring the needs of government and businesses are more closer aligned is only part of the solution; closer ties with universities and other educational institutions is just as important.

Long-term planning around education, talent, health and enterprise are essential "must haves" for the booming nations of tomorrow. Long-term infrastructure planning is absolutely critical and should be underpinned by a strategic focus on clusters, regenerating regions of the UK with high unemployment levels and offering rewards to corporates who help. The mind-boggling confusion over policy regarding airports highlights the challenge. Joined-up thinking on long-term solutions to address the UK's connectivity and capacity are urgently needed.

Finally, to compete globally, Britain needs an open market that attracts, retains and develops the best talent. It can only do so by encouraging businesses that are nimble, flexible and accommodating to their employees' changing demands. Celebrating business success, rewarding role models and promoting increased trade are all small changes that could make a big difference to UK status as a trading powerhouse.

The pace of change in the global economy is quickening. If we stand still as a nation, we will fall behind. To thrive in this future, we must be prepared. We must focus on the long term, forge closer partnerships between business and government, strengthen links abroad and support the export success of our small and medium-sized businesses. In this way we can create prosperity for all.

Lord Davies was chief executive, and then chairman, of Standard Chartered Bank before becoming Minister of State for Trade, Investment and Small Business. He is now a partner in private equity firm Corsair Capital, along with other non-executive roles.

II

The Challenge of Inclusive Growth

TRADE UNIONS IN THE NEW ECONOMY

Roy Rickhuss

Government, industry and unions will need to change if the UK is to be globally competitive and create more good, productive and sustainable jobs. Trade unions must enter a period of meaningful modernisation to complete their part of the bargain.

The world of work is changing faster than ever. That presents a challenge, not only for government and industry but also for the millions of people in the UK who manufacture, build, service, create and care. It likewise presents a challenge for trade unions like my own—Community. How do we support workers facing this new economic reality? There are more small and micro businesses than ever; only 16% of private-sector workers are members of a union; and people are likely to change their job seven, eight, or even nine times throughout their working lives. For too many people, the reality of working life is one of insecure employment, relatively low pay and poor-quality work. The Smith Institute's "Making Work Better" project has examined a series of recent studies of work in the UK and estimates that around 12 million people are unhappy with some aspect of their employment—from anxiety about loss of job status to actually losing their job and lots more in between.

The Shadow Business Secretary, Chuka Umunna MP, has outlined the challenge of creating inclusive growth: how to generate broad-based success that enables all to contribute and to achieve their aspirations. If we want an economy that works for everyone, then an incoming Labour government will have to take an active approach to make sure it happens.

It's not just about government; industry has to show leadership too. Long-term thinking, collaboration and investment in people is the route to improving the UK's poor standing against other major economies in terms of productivity and GDP. It's also about trade unions—which have a moral and economic obligation to help their members and the country more widely to play a part in rebuilding the UK economy.

REPOSITIONING TRADE UNIONS

To meet that obligation trade unions must enter a period of meaningful modernisation—looking to the future rather than relying on the past. Attempting to encourage this, the last Labour government introduced the Union Modernisation Fund which supported projects to help unions modernise their structures and processes. While there were merits to supporting this kind of activity at the time, the change we must see from unions now needs to be about culture, language and approach. If we make these changes, then the structural developments that are required to ensure that unions can provide relevant and fresh services, that appeal to the millions of workers who are not in a union, will naturally follow.

Trade unions need to be more honest and recognise that the image of the trade union movement is not generally positive. Responsible trade unions are a force for good in the workplace and in communities. On a daily basis trade unions are making workplaces safer, smarter and stronger—helping businesses compete globally, delivering public services more efficiently and encouraging long-term thinking. Our problem is while this approach is recognised by those involved it does not reach beyond a very narrow section of industry and society more generally. For that to change, not only must we moderate our language, but we also need to promote the work we do in partnership with employers and be proud of the successes we share—many of which mean our members have been valued at work in some way.

MODERN INDUSTRIAL RELATIONS

If the UK is to be globally competitive and deliver public services in the most effective manner then that will require clear leadership from an incoming Labour government to ensure modern industrial relations are prevalent across our economy. In 1997, Labour established a Partnership at Work Fund which facilitated significant industry-level and workplace engagement between trade unions and employers. This initiative had a particularly positive impact in the manufacturing sector, which was under pressure at the time from emerging low-wage economies and currency pressures from being outside the Euro zone. However, it was not as successful as hoped. Following a lukewarm evaluation of the fund and a change in approach from many of the new trade union general secretaries elected in the early 2000s, the fund closed in 2004, with only a handful of strategic projects surviving.

The Partnership at Work Fund was an example of a non-legislative measure introduced by government to enhance productivity and indirectly modernise trade unions. For the last ten years since it was abolished, there has been very little to fill that gap and there must be a more active approach. There is an opportunity to do this by developing an overarching industrial strategy with sector-specific strands. This could not only provide a framework for collaboration between businesses and government, it could also drive co-operation within businesses, between company representatives and unions. A simple way government could further encourage this is by giving greater weighting in its consultations to responses that are submitted jointly by employers and unions.

An excellent example of how partnership working can happen organically and have a real impact occurred when the former Tata Steel plant in Redcar was mothballed in 2010 following the economic crisis. Community worked closely with the management of the plant to minimise the impact of the closure, helping to prevent compulsory redundancies. This helped secure a new owner and investment in the plant from Sahaviriya Steel Industries (SSI), a Thai firm that offered the hope of bringing steel making back to Teesside. Since SSI took over the plant, Community has worked to modernise the conditions of employment in an industry that witnessed little structural change around working conditions for many years. This was a challenging process, but as we now reach the other side of this endeavour, the union and SSI can feel vindicated by the approach taken over the last three years. When organisations are forced to respond to circumstances often beyond their control, coming together to work in partnership can transform the expected outcome.

EMPLOYEE ENGAGEMENT

Another area where the UK lags behind our global competitors is in employee participation, which in many ways is connected to the problems we face in terms of productivity. According to the European Participation Index, the UK has the worst record for employee participation in Europe. While the circumstances with SSI in Redcar show what can be achieved when reacting to a difficult situation, it seems wholly counterproductive that more employers in this country do not seem to want to engage more regularly with their employees or unions on matters that affect the business and the people who work in that business.

I've lost count of the times I've been involved in meetings with companies facing problems and a positive suggestion has emerged from the trade union "side" of the table which has led to jobs being saved, new work being won or more productive working practices being introduced. Sadly, this type of strategic engagement doesn't happen enough. It is clear that there needs to be a massive culture change across British industry to involve employees more closely in the businesses where they work. Through deeper engagement between employers and employees, businesses will be better able to tackle the issues that arise, seek out new business opportunities and fix problems before they happen.

AN ACTIVE INDUSTRIAL STRATEGY

The development of an active industrial strategy which fosters strategic, tripartite engagement between business, unions and government would ensure a long-term approach from employers. Ed Miliband often talks about the "race to the bottom"—competing with other countries as a low-skill, low-wage economy—and he is right to be concerned. It is a concern that employers tell me they share too. They feel that the current hands-off approach from government is hurting the UK economy.

Developing sector-specific industrial strategies is not only about crafting a plan for each sector, it is about ensuring that there is more effective use of the levers available to government in areas such as procurement, taxation and skills policy to support that plan. Procurement is probably the most frustrating aspect of the current hands-off approach from the coalition. If public-sector contracts can be weighted heavily towards company A, because of its lower price, as opposed to company B, which has slightly higher costs but will train more apprentices, then it is obvious there is a structural problem within our procurement policy. This creates a false economy, saving small amounts in the context of government spending while at the same time storing up bigger issues for the future, such as skills shortages, a lack of vocational opportunities for young people and the cost of state support for underemployed workers.

Yet, where decision makers are prepared to take a more measured approach, success can be found. Royal Strathclyde Blindcraft Industries (RSBi) is one of the country's leading examples of social enterprise, successfully combining commercial success with socially responsible practices—with disabled workers being the vast majority of its employees. Community works in partnership with the RSBi and the industrial relations are modern and constructive. The two partners have worked together to call on the Scottish Government to adopt a procurement initiative whereby buyers can reserve contracts for supported businesses under Article 19, an element of a 2004 European Union directive. This has since been used extensively to ensure employment and apprenticeship opportunities for disabled workers in RSBi. It has also led to the company being able to compete more effectively for contracts that are not reserved for companies like RSBi, because of the productivity gains achieved through this innovative procurement process.

Workplaces where employees feel secure, have opportunities for self-development, receive fair pay and feel valued are more likely to be high performing. These workplaces represent what inclusive growth might look like. People will be happier at work if they feel rewarded appropriately and secure in their employment. I hope they will be even happier if they are represented by a professional trade union that strives to support their journey through working life.

TRADE UNIONS AND INCLUSIVE GROWTH

To generate more inclusive growth, government, industry and unions will each need to change. We need an active government that drives improvements in industrial relations to engage employees, create sustainable employment opportunities and provide ongoing productivity improvements, with a procurement policy that recognises those prepared to invest in skills. We need industry to be prepared to take a longer-term view, to invest in skills and to work in partnership with their workforce and their representatives. Finally, we need a more responsible trade union movement that acknowledges we can reach new members—and represent our current members more effectively—by ensuring that our reputation is enhanced in society.

To deliver this final change, there needs to be strong leadership within the trade union movement. The need for change is best summed up by a long-standing member of Community:

> Somehow we must capture the goodwill of the British people all over again. We have to let the public see the better side of trade unionism—all the millions of hours of voluntary work that trade unionists do up and down the country, week-in, week-out.
>
> The way which we care for our sick and elderly workers, our pensioners, the way which we support our communities, welfare centres, social clubs and all sorts of facilities for young people; the way in which we help to run our town councils, sit on the bench of the nation's magistrates' courts and play a part in the cultural, artistic and religious life of the nation.
>
> The vast majority of trade unionists, like the rest of British people are hardworking, loyal and patriotic. Yet this is not the image the public has of a trade unionist. They see only the bawling, yelling, sloganising ranter, the work-shy, idle card playing, shop floor worker or striker.
>
> These false images have to be removed before it is too late, and we must use every technique in the book to bring about a change in the public's perception of who we are and what we do . . . to see the day when Britain's trade unionists are more influential than ever before—not because of the power they can employ—but because of the contribution they make to the life of the nation.

Those are the words of 94-year-old Bill Sirs—former General Secretary of one of Community's founding unions, the ISTC. I chose those words not just because of the sentiment and message that lies in them, but also to illustrate the scale of the challenge facing trade unions in being a voice for those who need to benefit from inclusive growth. Bill wrote those words in 1985 and little has changed in almost 30 years—that isn't an option for the next 30 years.

Roy Rickhuss is general secretary of Community.

A NEW DIRECTION FOR A MORE INCLUSIVE ECONOMY

Sir Charlie Mayfield

Technological change is transforming the workplace, driving higher productivity but risking greater polarisation. Building an economy that offers a future for all requires a different approach to business conduct and education, and more plural ownership structures.

Over the past year, it has become clear the UK economy has transitioned from recession to growth. The positive statistics mean real progress in life for all those finding jobs or winning new orders for their business. But we know that while our labour market has done well at getting and keeping people in work, it has its share of complex, thorny problems.

The setbacks in productivity the UK has suffered over the years since recession have left a large gap in the productivity of British workplaces compared to those of leading advanced economies. On average, an employed person will spend more of their waking hours at work than in any other activity. The workplace is therefore a crucial arena for social mobility. However, there is strong evidence that in the UK and other developed economies, the workplace is not fulfilling this purpose as well as it could. Data from the OECD suggests that the level of income inequality in the UK is high and growing.

These problems are not new and are independent of the economic cycle. They are about the way we develop and deploy the talents of people, so that they can make the greatest possible contribution to our economic performance. With rapid technological change, there is an opportunity to close the productivity gap and, in so doing, create the best possible platform for expanding opportunity, increasing equality and inclusiveness and raising living standards. But this cannot be taken for granted. It will depend on the choices we make about how to prepare people for the world ahead through education, and on how businesses are owned and run.

TECHNOLOGICAL CHANGE IS GOOD FOR PRODUCTIVITY, BUT IT IS RESULTING IN A MORE POLARISED LABOUR MARKET

Across history, technology has transformed productivity in industry after industry, from agriculture to transportation, manufacturing, communications and healthcare. The progress of the past gives grounds for optimism about the future. However, there are signs that technology might be weakening the effectiveness of work as a driver of social mobility.

The experience of the Sky News reporter I spoke with recently brings this point to life. A decade ago, he would have needed a sound engineer and a cameraman travelling with him to every corner of the world. Now he needs only an enhanced iPhone and a broadband connection to file his reports. But the one thing he can't do without is a driver.

For some people, technology is an enhancement to their work. For others, it is replacing their once-valued professions. Indeed, demand for higher-skilled, technology-enabled roles has grown significantly in recent years. In the last two decades, the number of high-skilled jobs in UK has risen by 2.3 million, and in some occupations, like design, engineering and architecture, employers are struggling to fill positions. Demand for low-skill roles has also grown, with 1.8 million more jobs in areas such as care, administration, machine operatives and leisure. Yet, over the same 20-year period, we have seen a significant decrease in demand for middle-skilled workers, with 1.2 million fewer jobs available for these largely "routine"-based roles.

The trend towards an "hour-glass" shaped labour market is expected to continue, as the routine nature of many middle-skilled occupations makes them especially vulnerable to automation. The predictions are for faster growth of higher- and lower-skilled jobs compared with middle-skilled jobs in the UK into the next decade. This, of course, is not uniquely a UK phenomenon—this "hollowing out" of the workforce can be seen in many other developed economies. In the US, for example, the share of middle-skilled roles fell by 14 percentage points—from 59% to 45%—between 1983 and 2012, while the share of low-skilled and high-skilled occupations both rose.

It is hard to predict exactly which of many rapidly advancing technologies in the fields of robotics and artificial intelligence will have the greatest impact on the workplace, but we can be sure that the impact will be profound. A recent study at Oxford University found that nearly half of US jobs could be susceptible to computerisation over the next two decades, including higher-skilled, white collar occupations. Such predictions about the future are far from certain to occur, but it is wise to consider, at least, a world in which technology could lead to an intensification of inequality and the hourglass would become more exaggerated still.

Job polarisation matters for all range of reasons, most crucially for the limitations it may place on social mobility. If the trend continues, fewer middle-skilled occupations would mean less opportunity for low-skilled workers to progress, removing the next "rung" in the ladder of aspiration. A central social purpose of the workplace—to help people get on in life—may become harder to achieve.

TIME FOR A NEW DIRECTION

How can we address this risk of polarisation, and avoid the economic as well as social consequences that would result? There is no single, simple solution. But I believe we can take the first steps towards a more inclusive and equal economy by focusing on three areas: first, rethinking the way businesses conduct themselves and the choices they make in the use of technology; second, considering the role of education in supporting this; and third, encouraging greater plurality in the ownership structures of businesses. These are practical steps that will, over time, make a real difference.

Conduct

Let's take the first of these measures, conduct. An inclusive, sustainable economy relies on the conduct of its businesses, especially with respect to technology. Businesses can make choices about how they incorporate new technologies into their workplace. They can employ technology in ways that diminish—or even replace—the skills of the workforce. Alternatively, they can deploy technologies to complement and enhance the contribution of their employees. Not only is this more sustainable, but it is also more inclusive. While two companies may be selling the same product, the way the businesses deploy technology and the skills mix they nurture as a result, may be very different.

Let me give an example. In John Lewis we have one of the largest in-house delivery teams in the country. With a massive increase in demand for delivery, we have deployed technology to increase efficiency, such as deliveries per hour. But alongside that, we have trained and equipped our delivery drivers so they are becoming audio and TV technicians and appliance installers. Combinations of job design, technology and skills development can drive customer satisfaction, efficiency and pay.

Education

Conduct goes hand-in-hand with the second measure—education. Companies frequently complain about the shortage of skilled workers. But all too often, the burden is placed solely on schools and universities to fill this gap. We've got to look at how all parts of the system can pull in the same direction, and how employers can play their full part.

With over 40% of young people now going to university, it should be a major concern that many university degrees are not aligned to employers' needs. To fix this problem, we need much greater collaboration between our schools, universities, businesses and government—working together to prepare people for the roles employers need.

Working lifetimes have increased in length by a fifth, creating the possibility for four generations of people to work side-by-side. For many, career progression used to be based on getting better at doing the same thing. As people work longer, and technology cycles turn faster, it is crucial that workers, and workplaces, become more agile.

That requires linking-up work and education more effectively over the course of a working lifetime, so that it is unimaginable to find one without the other. We must rid our economy of the myth that education stops at the age of 21. After all, over 80% of those who will make up the workforce in a decade's time are already in employment.

Ownership

The final piece to the puzzle is ownership. While the plc remains the "norm" in both the British and international markets, employee-owned businesses represent a compelling alternative. When Spedan Lewis founded the John Lewis Partnership as an employee-owned business, he introduced a structure where "labour employs capital"—a radical inversion of the prevailing norm. A greater plurarity of ownership would promote social mobility within a more inclusive style of capitalism.

Employee ownership is of course not a panacea, and it is not suitable for every business, but it has key strengths, which are demonstrated in outperformance against other models of ownership. This is particularly true of knowledge-intensive businesses, where the majority of new jobs are expected to be created over the next ten years.

Evidence shows that other alternative forms of ownership also have striking results. Research by Boston Consulting Group and published in *Harvard Business Review* in 2012 demonstrated that family-owned businesses outperform their "conventionally" owned counterparts over the business cycle. In fact, over 30% of all firms generating more than $1 billion in revenues are in some form of family ownership.

Alternative forms of business ownership are gaining strength across the UK. Increased support to raise awareness, simplify legal models and introduce new tax reliefs has already created momentum towards real change in the number of collaborative and employee-owned businesses.

BUSINESS AND INCLUSIVE PROSPERITY

This is a critical moment for business leaders, and for champions of a more balanced and plural economy, to step up and support the movement for change. Over the longer term, technological change offers an opportunity for the UK economy to close the productivity gap, and to make the workplace once again a route to social mobility. But this is far from inevitable. Indeed, if current trends continue, technological change will exacerbate the problems of a polarised labour market.

To counter these trends, we must take a different approach. With deliberate action—in the conduct of businesses, in our approach to education and in the ownership structures we encourage and support—we can build an economy that is more productive and more inclusive.

Sir Charlie Mayfield is the chairman of John Lewis Partnership and the UK Commission for Employment and Skills.

BUSINESS AND GOVERNMENT WORKING TOGETHER FOR MORE INCLUSIVE GROWTH

Sir Peter Rigby

Creating good jobs for all requires an environment that respects and supports business success, and real partnership between business and government. LEPs should be merged into fewer, larger "Super LEPs" and given the powers and resources to succeed.

What does success look like in generating more balanced, sustainable and inclusive growth? The answer is that it gets people into work, irrespective of social group. People in good jobs are generally happier and healthier and can finance themselves, rather than put pressure on the state's finances.

This is the perfect end goal. If only the means of achieving this Nirvana were as easy as setting out the destination. Getting people into work sounds easy but has proved a most challenging task for generation upon generation.

BUSINESS NEEDS MORE CONSIDERATION

I believe the key to success is real partnership between business and local authorities, where business is encouraged to lead. Successive governments have introduced a veritable medley of regional structures and partnerships, designed to engage (and allegedly empower) regional business, local government and communities, in the name of creating jobs for all.

The current version of this approach is the Local Enterprise Partnership, or LEP—where I have three years' experience of chairing one. I believe LEPs have the potential to evolve and make a real difference, if the will to make it happen is there. It will depend on critical developments in LEP structure itself, which I will come to. But it will also depend on changes to the broader environment in which the partnership between business and government takes place. It is this broader environment that I will address first.

Successful partnership must begin with greater respect for the fact that business creates the jobs that everyone needs. This isn't a local or regional issue—it demands a national campaign to change public perceptions. There is a fundamental imbalance between the public perception of business and the people who own and run successful ones.

It is not a sin to be successful in business and, indeed, to generate wealth. Whilst most countries appreciate and respect successful entrepreneurs and business leaders, Britain has yet to learn to do so. In markets that are global our overseas, competitors value highly our people and facilities and are looking to recruit the education, skills, creativity and tenacity of British technicians, managers and senior executives. It is imperative that we fight to not only retain their skills and services but also transform the overall environment in which we operate.

If business is going to contribute fully in business-led engagement with local government, then there must be recognition, reward and compensation to attract successful and effective business people. So in addition to resetting public perceptions, a successful future partnership between business and government requires a healthy, sensible tax regime at both personal employment and corporate levels. Growth will come from established businesses and inward investment, with the bulk coming from organic growth across both domestic and export markets. It is vital to support local businesses in parallel with attracting inward investment. Companies will not invest unless the tax regime encourages investment. Entrepreneurs and investors need good returns and rewards on their effort, skills and investments.

Behind this, there is also an urgent need to realign and re-skill our educational system to complement business needs. Britain has fallen well behind its competitors in terms of literacy and numeracy, in focused further education and university education—all of which are critical to opportunity, employment and a good quality of life. This means a stronger emphasis on sciences and engineering, business-led management skills, languages and an appreciation of the work ethic, energy and enthusiasm essential to succeeding in the workplace and in business.

THE NEED FOR "SUPER LEPs"

Having addressed improvements that are needed to the general business environment to allow business to contribute more towards the goal of inclusive growth, I now turn to the specific issues for the future of LEPs. At root, their success depends on true empowerment. The success of partnerships between business and local government will stand or fall on how serious the ruling party—or should I say the Civil Service—is about handing over money and power.

Today, LEPs succeed against the odds. They were born with no structure, no strategy, no best practice or process, no money and no financial incentives to proactively recruit good people. That any have succeeded to date is down to the selfless determination and commitment from those who have stepped forward out of philanthropic motives. With sincere intent, they can really fly. To have a real impact, LEPs must have financial independence, respect and the power to cross local authority boundaries. Without any intervention, supply and demand will naturally dictate infrastructure requirements. Future LEPs can only hope to increase economic growth and jobs for all if they have the ability to align infrastructure and skills—untrammelled by political boundaries, crippling planning processes and a grand-national course to complete to get government money.

So let's imagine we have travelled forward in time 3–5 years. We have a real and effective partnership between government and business, through a smaller number of larger LEPs. Let's call them "Super LEPs." Super LEPs are more regionalised and led by leaders or elected mayors with the skills, remit, authority and purpose to drive real regional growth. Not only are the private and public sectors united in delivering economic prosperity, but they also have financial independence and are recruiting the best people at the market rate.

In this new world, there is a growing respect and appreciation that without business there are no jobs. This translates into a business-led supply and demand strategy around infrastructure. The Super LEPs work together on planning, transport and skills to optimise private-sector investment, create new employment floor space and—most important of all—increase the number of good jobs created.

Businesses connect easily with local government to access funding and support through a single point of contact. A customer-facing team sits in each "Super LEP" and finds out what local businesses need to grow. It then provides help to secure the right combination of business support, funding, planning, recruitment and skills to give them the best possible chance of growing quickly.

With Super LEPs empowered and resourced to succeed, business people at all levels are engaged with the Super LEPs and inspired to put back into their communities by the ease of engagement and awareness of recognition and reward.

Too good to be true? I don't believe so, if there is a serious will to make it happen. Because—to end where I began—it is what it takes to succeed in generating more balanced, sustainable and inclusive growth.

Sir Peter Rigby is founder, chairman and chief executive of Rigby Group PLC, one of the UK's largest leading privately owned businesses, and he chaired the Coventry and Warwickshire Local Enterprise Partnership.

SMART AND INCLUSIVE GROWTH

Mariana Mazzucato

Countries and regions that have been successful at innovation led "smart" growth have always had active state directed policies. Rather than worrying about picking or not picking winners, we should worry more about how such "directionality" is done, and how to make sure that the inevitable failures which choices around innovation always entail can be covered by some of the upside returns of the successes. This requires a new way of understanding public policy.

Innovation-led, "smart" and inclusive growth is imperative for a nation's success. Systems and eco-systems of innovation are needed so that new knowledge and innovation can diffuse throughout an economy. They require the presence of dynamic links between the different actors and institutions (firms, financial institutions, research/education, public-sector funds, and intermediary institutions), as well as horizontal linkages within organisations.

What, however, has not been given enough attention is the exact role that each actor in the system plays along the bumpy and complex risk landscape.[1] Is it the case that because some actors are investing in high-risk uncertain capital intensive areas, without sufficient recognition, other actors have been able to invest less, and yet capture a rising share of the rewards?

Developing an accurate understanding of the conditions necessary for the innovation eco-system to flourish is therefore needed. This includes a proper acknowledgment of the state's role in the collective system of innovation. If wealth-creating activity is to translate into raising living standards for all, the system needs to be symbiotic, not parasitic. Asking questions around the distribution of risks and rewards is essential if we want to achieve growth that is not only "smart" but also "inclusive."

RISK AND REWARDS IN INNOVATION

A key problem is that the underlying framework which justifies public investments does not explicitly consider risk-taking by the public sector in the entrepreneurial sense. Talk of the public sector simply "de-risking" or "facilitating" business-sector innovation misses the way in which public funds have actively shaped and created new markets rather than just fixed existing ones.

Market failure theory discusses "risk" in terms of the wedge between private and social returns, which may arise from the public goods or different types of positive and negative externalities. This is the classical argument that justifies state spending on basic research. However, the mission-oriented investments which resulted in most of the "general purpose technologies" cannot be understood within the market failure perspective. Missions, from putting a man on the moon to tackling climate change, involve investments along the entire innovation chain not only in classical "public good" areas. Such mission-oriented direct investments have created new technological opportunities, which are the key drivers affecting business investment. It is for this reason that we tend to see a higher business spend on R&D in countries with a higher public spend.

Mission-oriented public investments are not driven by the private/social "wedge," but by direct objectives of government—in areas like health, defense, energy or the pursuit for competitive superiority in areas like ICT. They involve not only horizontal investments in research and skills, and investments in "public goods" (all crucial) but also direct high-risk investments in particular companies and specific technologies. In other words, investment *along the entire innovation chain*: basic research, applied research, and early stage seed finance. For example, the US Small Business Innovation Research Programme (SBIR) has been key in providing patient, long-term committed finance to companies like Compaq and Intel. More risk-averse and increasingly short-termist private venture capitalists did not. Indeed, as private venture capital has become increasingly short-termist, with returns sought in 3 years (innovation can take up to 20!), mainly through IPO or buyout "exits," the only type of "long-term patient" capital that innovative firms can find is often through the public sector. Such public investments take the form of direct grants or loans, including guaranteed loans like the ones given recently to both Tesla Motors and Solyndra. One succeeded; one failed. As any venture capital (VC) investor will admit, most investments in innovative companies fail. But what's true for private VC that does not hold for government is the way in which the profits earned from the winning investments (e.g., Genentech for Kleiner Perkins) can more than cover the losses, and the funds needed for the next round of investment. Why did none of the upside from Tesla's success come back to government to fund the Solyndra loss?

Economists usually argue that the return to government is through tax. But is the current tax system working in a way that allows such socialisation of both risks and rewards? If not, should government consider more direct stakes in its investments to ensure a sort of revolving fund whereby the wins can fund the losses? This question is obviously less relevant for investments in general public good areas, like education and basic research, where we assume the benefit comes back through different types of spillovers. But it matters for the directed public venture capital types of investments that governments have been making and continue to make. I argue that because we do not have an economic framework that admits that active risk-taking entrepreneurial role for government, we have ended up socialising the risk, but privatising the rewards of such direct investments. Today, this is putting the innovation eco-system at risk and fueling inequality. The state has not been able to do what venture capitalists have: fund the downside with some of the profits from the upside, and use the remainder to fund the next round of investments. It is unrealistic to think that the risk (and inevitable failures) involved in direct investments in particular firms and technologies can be covered simply via tax.

INNOVATION AND INEQUALITY

In a system where the risks of investing in innovation are socialised, "smart growth" does not result in "inclusive growth." Indeed, the long-term trend in modern capitalism has been one of increasing inequality between people, countries and regions, with deleterious consequences to societal welfare and environmental sustainability.[2] Some authors, such as Daron Acemoglu of MIT, argue that technological change is "skill biased," so that skilled personnel are rewarded above unskilled labour, which in the extreme is excluded from the system.[3] Yet what the "skill-biased technological change" fails to explain is where skills come from: in this theory, "skill" is an exogenous factor. Other authors, such as Jacob Hacker and Paul Pierson, have analysed the politics of "winner takes all," in which policies (e.g. capital tax breaks) make the rich richer, while squeezing the middle and labour classes.[4]

In the paper "The risk-reward nexus in the innovation-inequality relationship," co-authored with William Lazonick, we go one step further and identify the mechanisms behind "winners take all" policies, providing an alternative explanation that takes into account the generation of skills and knowledge.[5] We argue that the uncertain, cumulative and collective characteristics of the innovation process (which generates skills, knowledge and technical change) make possible a disconnection between risks and rewards. Often, actors (such as private venture capital funds and business managers) that contribute less than others (such as the state and workers) to the innovation process are able to reap a return on their investments that is higher than the risk they assumed. This leads to increasing inequality between different actors involved in the innovation process, because certain actors manage to position themselves at the point where the innovative enterprise generates financial returns (e.g., close to the final product market or to the financial market).[6]

If the state is so important for funding high-risk investments in innovation, and given the commonly accepted relationship between risks and returns in finance, more thinking is required on whether and how the state should earn back a more direct return on its risky investments. That is, rather than worrying so much about the "picking winners" problem, more thinking is needed about how to reward the winning investments so they can cover some of the eventual losses—which are inevitable, as innovation is so deeply uncertain.

TAX CONTRIBUTION

Many argue that it is inappropriate to consider direct returns to the state because the state already earns back for its investments, indirectly via the taxation system. There are four arguments against this reasoning: (1) tax evasion (legal and illegal) is common and realistically will not disappear; (2) taxes, such as capital gains, have been falling over the last decades, precisely through a false narrative about who the wealth creators are; (3) global movements of capital mean that the particular country or region funding the innovation might not reap the benefits in terms of local job creation; and (4) investments directed at companies and particular technologies pose a very different problem from those in the "basics," such as education, health and research. If the state is being asked to make such investments, it is necessary for it to cover its inevitable losses when those arise.

Apple computers is a case in point.[7] Apple received its early stage funding from the US government's SBIR programme, and all the technologies which make the iPhone "smart" are also state funded: the internet, GPS, touchscreen display and the latest voice-activated SIRI personal assistant. Indeed, even Google's algorithm was funded by the state (through the National Science Foundation).

Yet both Apple and Google have employed commonly used accounting practices, which have resulted in a much lower tax bill for
the US government. It has been reported that, in order to avoid
taxes, Apple formed a subsidiary in Reno, Nevada, where there is
no corporate income or capital gain tax.[8] Creatively naming the
company "Braeburn Capital," Apple used it to channel a portion of
its US sales, instead of including them in the revenues it reported in
California, where its headquarters are located.

Apple reportedly saved $2.5 billion in taxes with this scheme—a
very large number, given the $9.2 billion state deficit California
experienced in 2009. In other words, the entire state budget deficit
would have been significantly reduced (by more than 25%) if Apple
had fully reported its US revenues in the state where a significant
portion of its value (discovery, design, sales, marketing, etc.) was
created and achieved. These facts simply reinforce that the tax system is not one that can be relied on for recouping investments in
risky innovation. Avoiding taxes or promoting share-buybacks programmes (as announced by Apple in April 2013) are the symptoms
of Apple's embracing shareholder-value ideology, which resulted in
the adoption of a new financialised business model.

Reinforcing or reforming the tax system is therefore a solution
for a red herring. The real problem is changing the way we talk
about the innovation economy, so that some actors are not able to
hype up their role and lobby for reductions in their tax contribution.
The hype behind the role of venture capital allowed the National
Venture Capital Association to convince US Congress to lower the
capital-gains tax rates from almost 40% in 1976 to as low as 20% in
the early 1980s. Similarly, in the UK, the Labour government in
2002 reduced the time that private equity has to be invested from 10
years to 2 years in the name of creating more finance for innovation.
This only increased short-termism and inequality rather than investments towards innovation. Thus we should focus on not only ar-
guing for a higher capital-gains tax (or Piketty's policy reforms
around the global wealth tax) but also creating a different story
about the real drivers of innovation.

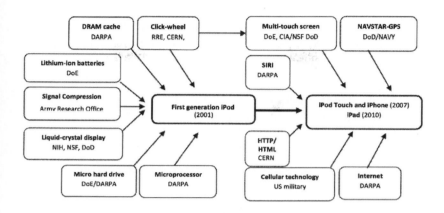

Figure 7.1. Government-Funded Technologies that Make Apple's iPhone "Smart" (Mazzucato, 2013, p. 109)

REAPING BACK A (DIRECT) RETURN

Where technological breakthroughs have occurred as a result of targeted state interventions, there is potential for the state to reap some of the financial rewards by retaining ownership over a small proportion of the intellectual property created. This is not to say the state should ever have exclusive license or hold a large proportion of the value of an innovation to the point of deterring more widespread application. The role of government is not to run commercial enterprises, but rather to spark innovation elsewhere. Nevertheless, government should explore whether it is possible to own some of the value it has created. Over time, this could generate significantly higher value and then be reinvested into growth generating investments.

There are various possibilities for considering a direct return to the investing state. One is to make sure that state loans and guarantees do not come without strings attached. Loans as well as grants could have conditions, like income contingent loans, similar to that of student loans. When a company makes profits above a certain threshold after it has received a loan/grant from the state, it should be required to pay back a portion. This is not rocket science, but it goes against some deep-seated assumptions. Currently, with budget deficits under so much pressure, it is no longer possible to ignore the issue.

There is also the possibility of the state retaining equity in the companies that it supports. This does occur in some countries, such as Israel through the Yozma public venture capital fund, or in Finland, where SITRA, a public funding agency, retained equity in its early stage investments in Nokia. Of course, equity stakes are also retained by state investment banks, such as China Development Bank and KfW, which are two lead investors in the emerging green economy.[9] But state equity in private companies is suspect in countries like the US and the UK for fear that the next step is . . . communism. And yet the most successful capitalist economies have had active states, making such risky investments, and we have been too quick to criticise them when things go wrong (e.g., Concorde) and too slow to reward them when things go right (e.g., the internet).

It is indeed curious that even when there are explicit agreements that would allow government to retain a share, it shies away from doing so. In 2010 the US Federal Government loaned $465 million to Tesla Motors. Tesla paid off the loan in 2013. The loan granted the government a warrant to buy 3 million stocks at less than $8 per share. Yet, when Tesla paid off the loan in 2013, stocks were trading at $93 per share. At this point, the government warrant was worth about $280 million; yet the government lost the right to have shares simply because the loan was paid back. This ignores the fact that the government, even if paid back, risked immensely that Tesla would finish like Solyndra. Government is not just a "spender" or "facilitator" but also a high-risk "investor," and it should be rewarded for supplying long-term, high-risk funds in an "eco-system" where the private financial sector doesn't.

Similarly, why is it that government has never exercised its official right to put a cap on drug prices when the drugs in question are publicly funded? It is the lack of a complete understanding of how the state contributes to radical innovation that is putting pressure on it to not claim its share—for the tax payers who bear the highest risk.

Thus, more thinking is needed about how to reward winning public investments so they can both cover some of the eventual losses. We also need to rethink how public investments are accounted in the national income accounting. Investments in innovation are different than current expenditures. The latter does not add to balance-sheet assets; the former does and is potentially productive investment in the sense that it creates new value. When setting limits to fiscal deficits, it is therefore necessary to distinguish public debt contracted for investment in R&D and infrastructure (value-creating investments) from public debt contract for (public or private) consumption. In this sense, financial and accounting reforms should be regarded as an essential pre-requisite for any successful smart and inclusive growth plan.

REWARDING GOVERNMENT

Understanding the state as lead risk-taker opens the question about how such risk-taking can reap back a return. While many have been quick to blame the government when it fails to "pick winners," they have been much less quick to reward it when it succeeds. A framework is required for understanding better both risk-taking and how collective systems of innovation map into systems of rewards. Getting the balance right will make the objective of smart and inclusive growth less about spin, and more about concrete mechanisms.

Mariana Mazzucato is RM Phillips professor in the economics of innovation at Sussex University.

NOTES

1. Mazzucato, M. (2013). *The Entrepreneurial State: Debunking the Public vs. Private Myth in Risk and Innovation*: Anthem Press.

2. See Wilkinson, Richard G., & Pickett, Kate. (2009). *The Spirit Level: Why Greater Equality Makes Societies Stronger*. New York: Bloomsbury; Piketty, T. (2014). *Capital in the Twenty-First Century*. Cambridge, MA: Harvard University Press.

3. Acemoglu, D. (2002). Technical Change, Inequality, and the Labor Market. *Journal of Economic Literature, 40*(1), 7–72.

4. Hacker, J. S., & Pierson, P. (2011). *Winner-Take-All Politics: How Washington Made the Rich Richer—and Turned Its Back on the Middle Class*. New York: Simon and Schuster.

5. Lazonick, W., & Mazzucato, M. (2013). The risk-reward nexus in the innovation-inequality relationship: Who takes the risks? Who gets the rewards? *Industrial and Corporate Change, 22*(4), 1093–1128.

6. Mazzucato, M. (2013b). Financing innovation: Creative destruction vs. destructive creation. *Industrial and Corporate Change, 22*(4), 851–867.

7. Lazonick, W., Mazzucato, M., & Tulum, Ö. (2013). Apple's changing business model: What should the world's richest company do with all those profits? *Accounting Forum, 37*(4), 249–267.

8. Duhigg, C., and Kocieniewski, D. (2012). How Apple Sidesteps Billions in Taxes. *The New York Times*, iEconomy Series. April 28.

9. See Mazzucato, M., & Shipman, A. (2014). Accounting for productive investment and value creation. *Industrial and Corporate Change* (forthcoming).

III

The Innovation Imperative

INNOVATION AND GROWTH: A ROADMAP FOR THE NEXT GOVERNMENT

Lord David Sainsbury

Focusing on addressing clear weaknesses in our national system of innovation must be a key priority for a government that supports a more entrepreneurial and dynamic model of competition.

In recent years, neoclassical economists have defined economics as being the study of how to allocate scarce resources among competing uses. In 1932 the British economist Lionel Robbins summed up this view in the following words:

> Whatever Economics is concerned with, it is not the causes of material welfare as such . . . Economics is the science which studies human behaviour as a relationship between ends and scarce means which have alternative uses.

In this static view of competition, which is totally different from the world in which most entrepreneurs see themselves working, a nation's factors of production are fixed, and markets allocate them to where they will produce the greatest return. But in a more realistic and entrepreneurial view of competition, as well as markets allocating scarce resources, firms seek to increase their profitability through developing new products and processes. Instead of deploying a fixed pool of factors of production, firms and nations seek to improve the quality of factors, raise the productivity with which they are utilised and create new ones.

If the ability of firms to increase their productivity by innovating and upgrading themselves in competition with foreign firms is seen as the primary source of a country's rate of economic growth, then the accumulation of organisational and technological capabilities by firms must become a central concern of policymakers. If we want to develop policies to help industry grow, we need to understand how firms in some countries are able to accumulate organisational and technological capabilities faster than in others, thereby creating new and more productive opportunities for investment, as well as how financial and labour markets in those countries do a better job of allocating resources to these more productive activities.

FOUR KEY ECONOMIC INSTITUTIONS

By looking at the record of economic growth in different countries, it is clear that four institutions which do not appear in neoclassical growth models play a key role in these two processes. They are the institutions which underpin a country's financial and labour markets, its corporate governance system, its education and training system and its national system of innovation, which is defined as the network of institutions in the public and private sectors whose activities and interventions initiate and diffuse new technologies.

This may seem like a very academic debate, but if the government is seeking to develop policies which will help industry grow and be more profitable, this issue is a key one. If one believes in the neoclassical model of the economy, then the only role of government is to make labour and capital more flexible, including making it easier for firms to make workers redundant, to incentivise entrepreneurs by cutting tax rates and to reduce the costs of companies, such as by creating enterprise zones.

If, on the other hand, one believes that the more entrepreneurial and dynamic view of competition that I have described is more realistic, as well as making certain that financial and labour markets are allocating labour and capital resources to the places where they will produce the greatest returns, governments need to make certain that the four key economic institutions I have mentioned are operating effectively.

There are, of course, neoliberals who will agree that institutions are important, but who will argue that these should be allowed to evolve naturally without government involvement. But there are two good reasons why they need to get involved. In the case of institutions which underpin a country's financial and labour markets and its corporate governance system, the government has to get involved to resolve conflicting interests. In the case of a country's national system of innovation and its education and training system—the "soft infrastructure" of capitalism—it has to get involved before it has to provide these public goods resources which industry needs in order to build competitive advantage and added value in global markets.

THE "RACE TO THE TOP"

If one looks at economic growth and innovation from this new perspective, then all countries today are involved in what I think is best described as a "Race to the Top." As a result of the collapse of communism, China's shift to a market economy and India's dismantling of its command-and-control economy, 1.5 billion new low-paid workers entered the world's labour market, almost exactly doubling it.

The only way that developed countries can compete in this new global economy is by getting out of low value-added industries which are labour intensive and do not require highly skilled workers, such as cheap textiles, and getting into high value-added industries where innovation and a highly skilled workforce are of critical importance, such as the IT industry, aerospace and pharmaceuticals. Hence the importance of science, technology and innovation.

Thomas Friedman argued in his book, *The World Is Flat*, that because of advances in ICT technologies, people anywhere in the world can innovate and compete on equal terms. But the world of innovation is very spiky. Innovation is concentrated to an extraordinary extent in places like Silicon Valley, Bangalore and Cambridge, where the institutions are supportive of innovation. The government must, therefore, make certain that our national system of innovation is fit for purpose.

STABLE INDUSTRY POLICY

To improve our economic performance, it is vitally important not to take the "ground zero" approach taken by too many parties in opposition, whereby the incumbent government's policies are written off in favour of a radical overhaul. This is disastrous because good policies get swept away with bad policies. Introducing new policies and getting them to work takes time, and in the meantime the performance of companies suffers.

This point will be of particular importance at the next General Election because the last Labour Government introduced a whole range of policies in the field of science and innovation, including the Technology Strategy Board, the Higher Education Innovation Fund, R&D tax credits, the Small Business Research Initiative and the Patent Box. These policies have been largely successful, and to their great credit the Coalition Government—with the exception of the abolition of the Regional Development Agencies—has maintained them. As a result, UK industry and science have experienced 15 years of stable and consistent policies, the value of which cannot be over-estimated.

A ROADMAP FOR THE NEXT GOVERNMENT

Where, then, should the next government focus its efforts? There are three areas where action is required.

First, we need a new 10-year plan for the funding of science that sees a steady increase in the amount allocated to basic research and also restores a stream of capital spending. If Research Councils and other funding bodies are able to plan ahead, resources will be used much more efficiently. And while it probably once made sense to cut back on capital spending, if cuts had to be made in a period of austerity, if a stream of capital funding were not restored soon, the lack of modern facilities would start to impact the quality of scientific research.

Secondly, a major achievement of the last Labour Government was to greatly improve the amount of knowledge transfer from universities to industry, mainly as a result of the Higher Education Innovation Fund, which helps universities to invest in initiatives to engage with industry. As a result, the level of knowledge transfer from our universities is as good as that of American universities in most cases. But more could be done to improve the commercialisation of research. More money should be allocated to the Technology Strategy Board (TSB) for the setting up of Innovation Platforms. By bringing together organisations focused on a particular social challenge, such as intelligent transport systems and services, assisted living or low-carbon vehicles, Innovation Platforms enable the integration of a range of technologies along with better co-ordination of policy, regulations, standards and procurement. There are plenty more areas where they could be put in place to help with the commercialisation of new technologies. The amount of money going to the TSB for generic technologies should also be increased, in order to narrow the "valley of death" that small high-tech companies face when introducing new products or services based on cutting-edge technologies.

Furthermore, to help with the process of commercialisation of research, the R&D expenditures of government departments, which have been run down by the Coalition Government in recent years, should be re-established, ring-fenced and used more effectively to support innovation in the industries which government departments sponsor. A striking feature of the US national system of innovation is the way that government departments use targeted resources of scientific and technological research to advance new technologies in the business community, whereas in the UK, there have only been a few attempts to replicate this success, such as the creation of the Office for the Strategic Co-ordination of Health Research by the Department of Health and the support given by the Ministry of Defence to its contractors. There are a number of areas, such as energy, water and the agri-food industries, which make an important contribution to UK industry, and which could benefit massively from government departments supporting innovation in them.

The third area where a future government should focus its efforts is the technological dimension of regional policy. There is an urgent need to support the growth of new industries in the less prosperous regions of the UK. The abolition, rather than reform, of the Regional Development Agencies (RDAs) was a mistake, and the Regional Growth Fund—which partly replaced the RDAs—has achieved very little.

We need to find a way, possibly through City Deals, to support high-tech clusters in the regions and to implement the recommendations in Andrew Witty's excellent report, "Encouraging a British Invention Revolution," on the role that universities can play in supporting new industries in the knowledge economy.

A huge amount of innovation takes place in clusters of companies, and always has done. The cotton industry at the time of the industrial revolution wasn't spread across the country, but rather centred in Manchester in the same way that the car industry was centred initially in Detroit. Why is this the case? The answer can be found in the linkages, complementarities and spillovers of technology, skills, information, marketing and customer needs that are the basis of competitive advantage and essential for innovation and the growth of productivity.

Governments cannot create clusters, but when they exist they can support them and remove barriers to their growth. A recent report by the Centre for Cities and McKinsey shows, for example, that most of the key clusters in the UK have major infrastructure issues which the government needs urgently to tackle. National policies, such as knowledge transfer from universities and incentives for venture capital, can also support the emergence of clusters. But the government needs to organise itself to support clusters effectively. The government should appoint a Minister in the Department for Business, Innovation and Skills with a clear responsibility for supporting clusters, and for getting other departments to do so. In addition, the government, as part of its regional policy, should make available extra funds to the Technology Strategy Board to support technology projects in regional clusters.

If political parties want to win the votes of industrialists and scientists, these are the sort of policies, focused on addressing clear weaknesses in our national system of innovation, they should support.

Lord David Sainsbury is a member of the UK House of Lords and former UK Minister of Science and Innovation. He is the author of *Progressive Capitalism: How to Achieve Economic Growth, Liberty and Social Justice*.

THE POWER TO CREATE

Matthew Taylor

We need industrial policies that help strengthen and grow the UK's world-leading creative sector. This has to paired with a recognition of the links between cultural flourishing and social and economic progress.

Creativity is often seen as an attribute of certain activities and industries. Fourteen industries such as architecture, fashion and publishing comprise a creative sector that in 2012 contributed £71.4 billion to the UK economy and employed 1.68 million British people. This sector has achieved the fastest growth of any UK sector in 2012. Our status as world leaders in design, arts and television brings clear economic benefits as well as being a cause for celebration in its own right. Indeed, the Royal Society for the encouragement of Arts, Manufactures and Commerce (RSA), of which I am chief executive, argues strongly for the links between cultural flourishing and social and economic progress.

Yet by focusing on creativity in a growing but discrete section of the economy, we lose sight of another account of creativity—one that is more universal and democratic. The RSA is starting to explore how the creative life, too often confined to an elite or a sector, should be fostered throughout the economy and society. We are striving to realise the promise of mass creativity. We refer to this idea as the "Power to Create."

At the heart of the Power to Create is a philosophical commitment to the ideal that everyone should be the author of their own lives. While the first aspect of a creative life is individual freedom to think our own thoughts and make our own decisions, it requires positive freedom and resources to pursue our choices—not just hard resources but also the capabilities and knowledge to be free.

The aspiration of a creative life also requires recognition that "we are only individuals as much as we are social," as Richard Rorty has written. Our creations, whether performances, products or ideas, are grounded in and find meaning in the social relationships of which we are a part. Thus to prize creativity as a substantive virtue urges our commitment to a society in which this prize is realistically attainable not just for ourselves but also for our fellow citizens. The progressive mission is for what Roberto Unger describes as a "larger life" to be available for all.

CREATIVITY TIPPING POINT?

Is there any reason to believe the Power to Create is anything other than a distant aspiration? I believe there is. We are reaching a point at which the possibility of, and the need for, a creative citizenry looms before us and presents us with urgent choices.

An Increasing Supply of Creativity

The first changes are around human capability and appetite. In less than two generations we have gone from under 10% to almost half of young people experiencing higher education. While we might lag behind other countries in some areas, our young people are in the top quartile of developed nations when it comes to problem solving ability. RSA research shows more young people than ever before wanting the autonomy of owning their own business even though the returns and security are often lower than a traditional job, and among those opting for employment, a growing proportion say they make decisions influenced by the values and ethical practices of employers. Around the developed world, more people are making their life goal what the Word Values Survey calls "self-expression."

Technology is the second great engine of change. The internet has led to a step change in affordable easy access to key tools of creativity: learning, communicating, trading and collaborating. In music, films, photographs, blogs, apps and social networks hundreds of millions of people have generated content. Inexpensive platforms such as Etsy and Kickstarter have released waves of human creativity, entrepreneurial aspiration and collaborative endeavour. Peer-to-peer and sharing economy platforms, whether social enterprises like Streetbank or commercial like AirBnB, enable anyone to trade, blurring the boundaries between buyer and seller. Human trust and reciprocity are as important as digital algorithms to the success of these platforms.

Technology can reduce autonomy and dull creativity and as it becomes ever more central to our identities we need to have an explicitly political debate about who controls it and for what purpose. Nevertheless, in aggregate, across a wide spectrum of human activity, greater creativity is being enabled and encouraged. And as the rise of music festivals and the makers' movement show, while the relationship between creativity on and off line is unpredictable, it is also largely positive.

An Increasing Demand for Creativity

The third trend is the increasing demand for a creative citizenry in all sectors. Various factors, including the accelerating pace of change in markets, the need for continuous innovation, the expectation of more personalised service and the growing appetite for authenticity and emotional connection in products and services, all increase the premium on the capacity of employees to be creative and self-motivated.

Increasingly, the Government also wants creative citizens. In the face of complex problems and the impact of austerity forward thinking public agencies are recognising that their citizens and communities need to be seen as potential assets not just bundles of needs. As Simon Stevens head of NHS England said in June, "achieving change in the NHS is not merely a techno-rationalist activity, it's health as a social movement." Methods of service co-design and co-delivery are being pursued, again blurring the boundary between producer and consumer. Initiatives like Homeshare are modern examples of an old ideal—reciprocal civic relationships offering an alternative or adjunct to public services. Of course, huge challenges like caring for an ageing population, tackling inequality or responding to climate change require concerted action at national, local and international level, but our strategies will also require an adaptive and creative citizenry with the skills and confidence to develop its own solutions.

THE BARRIERS TO A CREATIVE SOCIETY

Culture

In our culture the idea that everyone can and should live creatively is not yet accepted as an aspiration let alone a practical imperative. 43% of the workforce, thirteen million people in the UK report that they are not using their skills at work. In assessing the value of education and employment, we still give a relatively low priority to autonomy, engagement and motivation.

A concrete symbol of limited commitment toward the ideal of creative lives for all is the persistence of educational privilege and inter-generational inequality ("the past devouring the future," in Thomas Piketty's memorable phrase). The point is not inequality per se, but that the concentration of wealth and opportunity means key resources that foster creative aspirations and choices are not distributed in the way most likely to maximise the benefits to society as a whole. If we judge social progress by the scale of human creativity, extreme inequality is deeply inefficient.

Not only is capital concentrated in certain strata of the population, it is concentrated in assets—like London house values—that do little to expand people's creative possibilities. Access to relatively small amounts of capital can have a much greater impact on people's sense of efficacy and opportunity than increases in income; yet a quarter of our adult population effectively has no capital. Some of the first casualties of austerity were initiatives—such as the child trust fund and the savings gateway—explicitly designed to address this deficit.

Institutions

The idea that one class is simply by its nature bound to rule another is seen as reactionary and even offensive but the assumption that only a certain strata of people, of learners, of workers, of places can be expected to be creative endures. So long and so deep has that assumption held sway that it is deeply inscribed into our society's institutions.

In the workplace, we assume that only a certain number of roles within the institution can be creative, and that an essential role of management systems is to sort posts and people into a pyramidal structure, with the most creative jobs at or near the top. Institutions often allocate each individual a role and separate this from the other multiple roles they occupy. We talk about the different interests of teachers, health workers and police officers on the one hand and parents, patients and citizens on the other, but most teachers are parents, all of us will need care at some time and we are all citizens. And institutions too often lose sight of substantive and ethical goals, instead prioritising organisational self-interest or—in the public sector—risk avoidance. As John Kay argues, when companies replace the goal of producing great products with maximising share value, they easily lose their way. When the only way to cope at work is to leave your identity, values and human sympathies at home in the morning, it is not surprising that people feel demoralised and jaded.

Most large organisations are trying to grapple with these institutional habits and their impact on their capacity to recruit, retain and motivate creative employees. Frederick Laloux cites Morning Star, the world's largest tomato-processing company, as an example of how these barriers can be overcome even in a capital-intensive business working to exacting standards in a traditional industry. Up to 2,400 employees each year run the company entirely on self-managing principles, according to which any "colleague" can make creative decisions, and rather than operating within a hierarchical pyramid, colleagues agree to honour commitments to each other. The best schools aren't just good at getting children through exams; they are also intelligent communities.

The Role of the State

As a goal, democratic creativity leads to a profound reconsideration of the role and working methods of the state. In some areas the state would do more than at present, and in others less.

Greater activism is needed in shaping the market and its outcomes. The creative state would ensure open markets with low barriers of entry and diverse forms of ownership: encourage and enforce permissive intellectual property regimes, demand that utilities and essential services—including the global internet giants—are run with the public interest at heart, invest in tomorrow's infrastructure (including new institutions which foster and grow innovation). As Eric Beinhocker and Nick Hanauer have recently argued, the greatest achievements of capitalism lie less in economic growth or profit but in helping find solutions to problems that matter to us. The answer is not reams of flawed regulation (which tends to become outdated as soon as it is implemented), but rather a new partnership between modern Government and enlightened business based on a shared commitment to a creative economy.

But as well as being more active in markets, the governors of the state—particularly the central state—need to be aware that its scale, complexity and accountability often make it badly suited to human scale interventions. Today's citizens, aspiring to greater self-determination, want a government that enables them to feel self-reliant, not one which creates and reinforces dependency. The creative society would seek to devolve power to the lowest effective level not just because the centre is too distant but also because we would encourage different places to do things in substantively different ways, not merely experiments in service delivery but also experiments in place shaping—indeed, experiments in living.

More profoundly the values and analysis behind the Power to Create encourages a questioning of the very idea of traditional policymaking. A new policymaking process that fostered mass creativity would see leaders articulating a clear vision as teachers and convenors, not as people who make decisions on our behalf. When it comes to social policy, politicians and managers need to replace the blunt tools of policymaking with those of design, in which continuous experimentation, learning by failing and co-producing with consumers and users are the norm.

SOCIAL JUSTICE AND THE ECONOMY

In the face of the economic stagnation and crises of the 1970s, a powerful neoliberal critique seemed to win the argument that state intervention and the pursuit of social justice and expanding public provision were incompatible with economic dynamism. In response, during the 1990s, modernisers like Bill Clinton, Tony Blair and Gerhardt Schroeder developed the argument the goals of social justice were compatible with—indeed, complementary to—a successful market economy and that, in turn, a dynamic economy enabled investment in measures to promote justice. Although intellectually more subtle, in practice this approach encouraged a view that as long as the economy was delivering growth, the method by which it did so and consequences of that method were largely irrelevant.

Thus the rise of speculative finance and the growth of market-generated inequality were largely ignored as long as the tax receipts kept on rolling in.

Following the 2008 credit crunch there was strong feeling that the nature of the economy itself required re-examining. The power of financial capitalism and the scale of extreme inequality were seen as critical problems, although not ones with ready solutions. The big question is whether it is possible to envisage an inclusive, sustainable, economy which contributes to progressive values not just through generating taxable surpluses but also through its very mode of operation. Partly spurred by austerity, there is also a recognition that social programmes cannot succeed unless they too—built into their operating systems—enable citizens to grow their individual and collective resilience and problem solving capacity. Furthermore, our traditional ways of thinking about politics, policy and social change are proving increasingly inadequate in the face of an ever faster moving and more complex world.

The "Power to Create" moves beyond an instrumental view of the economy, a paternalistic view of social policy and a mechanical model of policy. The radical reform of our economic, social and political institutions must be premised on the historical possibility, and the ethical imperative, of creative lives for all.

Matthew Taylor is chief executive of the Royal Society for the encouragement of Arts, Manufactures and Commerce (RSA).

WHAT THE INNOVATORS OF TOMORROW SEE TODAY

Billy Boyle

R&D is at the heart of disruptive technologies that have the potential to transform entire industries and create high-quality jobs. Government has to continue to fund hubs and clusters where global companies can be founded and raise the ceiling of aspiration for tomorrow's innovators.

As well as pouring my energy into the business I co-founded, Owlstone Nanotech, I'm a keen, albeit atrocious, runner. Earlier this year, Roger Bannister celebrated the 60th anniversary of breaking the four-minute mile. Before 6 May 1954, the vast majority of people thought it impossible. Within two months of Bannister's success, two more runners came in under the time. Ten years later, a seventeen-year-old school boy named Jim Ryun had run a mile in less than the magic four minutes. Physically, nothing had changed in these athletes over that time. But there had been a mental shift, a change in perception in what they believed to be possible. It was this that allowed them to succeed.

This story illustrates a broader point. We all define what we think is possible in part by looking at what those around us have been able to do. In order for our children to develop the ideas, technology and innovation to drive the business and economy of tomorrow, they have to believe that this is a world open to them, no matter where they come from.

Owlstone Nanotech develops chemical sensors that can be used in applications ranging from the detection of explosives to the detection of diseases, such as cancer. In the ten years since we founded the company, we have built a team of 45 people, raised over $20M of investment, and won $10M in US military contracts. I can look back over my own journey and pick out two moments which fundamentally shaped my view of what was possible for me.

"MAYBE I CAN GET INTO CAMBRIDGE?"

The technology at the heart of Owlstone was born in the basement lab of the Cambridge University Engineering Department, where I sat with my friends and co-founders, David Ruiz and Andrew Koehl. R&D is at the heart of disruptive technologies that have the potential to transform entire industries and create high-quality jobs. This is why Government should continue to invest heavily in it. As a city, as a hub for scientific research, as a place where global companies have been founded, Cambridge is a world leader and without it our company would not exist.

Let me take a step back to how I got to this great university in the first place. As a youngster growing up in West Belfast, only the second in his family to go to university at all, Cambridge was not on the radar; it was not something my teachers considered or what I thought possible for myself. It was not my teachers, but my elder brother who changed my perception, by applying to and getting into Cambridge. When I visited him at age 14, all my preconceptions about Cambridge being for posher, richer kids melted away. After all, he wasn't a toff; he was "just" my brother. I got a place to study engineering myself, and at Cambridge found the education, connections and inspiration to build my own business.

What was true for me stands for others too: access to education is a huge driver of social mobility, inclusive growth and personal fulfilment. Because of my experience, I decided to get involved with the Linacre Institute, a charity which aims to help Sixth Formers at comprehensive schools and colleges reach the UK's most competitive universities, where they are still staggeringly under-represented. I want to show them that I had come from a similar background and to change their perceptions: if they see that enough, they will know that they can break their own four-minute mile.

"MAYBE I CAN START MY OWN COMPANY?"

Roll forward from my undergraduate years, and a mental switch flicked in my brain as I sat in a Cambridge lecture theatre aged 24, watching two guys a year older than me describe how they had just been backed by a venture capital firm to take their technology from the laboratory bench to people's homes. I had grown up on the stories of kids starting companies in their garage, but here they were, not a book chapter but my peers taking a step down the path that I wanted to follow. A year later, Owlstone had raised $2M and I was invited back to give the lecture.

The common theme in these two stories is that by showcasing role models we can change people's perception of what is possible—and so raise their ceiling of aspiration. Across the technology community there are plenty of role models who want to pass the ball forward, to give time and to help where they can. We have to find ways to harness their experiences and their enthusiasm so that others can progress as they have. On the demand side, we have a generation of children who don't necessarily know what they are truly capable of. They might not see science and engineering as viable for them. They might not believe they can get into university, or have the right technical skills for an apprenticeship. We have to show them what is possible. Their creativity and talent have to be unleashed to fuel tomorrow's companies and power our economy.

Billy Boyle is co-founder and president of Owlstone Nanotech, Inc.

ENCOURAGING TECHNICAL INNOVATION AND HIGH-GROWTH SMES

John Davis

With the evolution of cloud technology, dynamic SMEs in the high-tech sector have a path-breaking opportunity to compete, not just with big businesses in the UK but also on an international stage.

How does a start-up get off the ground? With hard work, long hours, total commitment, guesswork, good advice, a solid support network and more. I could go on, but what it really boils down to is a few people working very hard, making difficult decisions and learning to fill a lot of roles all at once. This may sound basic, but it's often forgotten: they need all the support they can get.

In the last fifteen years, that is what I have been focused on, initially as MD of a Barclays subsidiary, Clearlybusiness, and then as marketing and product director at Barclays Business. Since 2011, I've been managing director of my own small business. BCSG is a fast-growing, now 100-strong company offering cloud solutions to small businesses through partnerships with corporates; more than 200,000 businesses have subscribed to our services in the last 3 years. So I'm a small business owner who has spent the last fifteen years trying to help small businesses.

Right now this is an exciting place to be. Cast your mind back to the turn of the century: dial-up internet connections, limited storage space, life before smartphones and social media. In those days, technical solutions were principally designed for big organisations and scaled down in an often clumsy, compromised way for their smaller competitors. These versions were usually too complicated, too expensive, or simply not fit for purpose. It kept the smaller business a little behind the curve and tied people who needed to be out and about to the office, to hard drives and filing cabinets. In addition, it tied them to specialists whose services they had to pay for.

DEMOCRATISATION AND NEW OPPORTUNITIES

With the evolution of the cloud and more reliable networks, we are seeing a levelling of the playing field. That's largely thanks to the tech sector, which is busy building apps that answer all sorts of small business needs (take a look at GetApp and you'll see over 5,500 listed).

One of their biggest benefits is that they are filling the skills gap. In the early days of my business, there were four people doing everything: answering phones, building relationships with clients, handling the post . . . Human resources was an area that we found difficult. Our experience was limited and we were growing so fast that our HR processes and procedures were not keeping pace with the business. Now there's an app for that—more than one, in fact.

These apps are hosted in the cloud, which means there is no significant upfront capital investment, just a monthly or annual fee. And people can log in from wherever they are, setting them free from their desks and reducing the need for after-hours admin. If it wasn't an over-used term, I would say the cloud is a small business revolution. It's making enterprises nimble, focused and competitive, so much that it can be hard to tell a small company from a big one.

Small business owners still need good, practical advice. Where can they get it? Business Link was closed in 2011. Business banks are having to cut back on their relationship managers. Accountants and financial advisers can go only so far with their help.

There is a world of words, videos and apps online, but who can small business owners trust? How will they find out about the things they don't yet know about? The things they don't even know they don't know? It is hard for them to get the kind of ongoing, wide-ranging guidance they need. Interestingly, this is an area that corporates like banks and telecom companies are just beginning to move into, with services that complement their core products. It is early days, though, and advice (and curated tools to supplement that advice) are still in seriously short supply.

TELLING A DIFFERENT STORY

And so is press coverage. Column inches are essential for fast-growing SMEs—to spread the word, attract new customers, bring new investment on board, establish the concept of start-ups in the public consciousness, garner support from unexpected areas. After all, half of all jobs in the UK come from these businesses. Their success is key to the economy. In the US, where my organisation is now building a presence, it seems that government and media are joined up in their celebration of and support for small businesses. Publications with a business readership, like Forbes.com, have a strong focus on the sector.

Here, it is a different story. Trying to get any UK coverage of SMEs activities is an uphill struggle. As a nation, our understanding of entrepreneurship seems to have stopped at Richard Branson—who is a national treasure, of course, but evidently no longer a small business person. Large corporates dominate the business coverage, all too often with a big-bad-business twist. Celebrating success for any business whether large, medium or small appears to be a step too far for the UK media at the moment. Imagine if they did: maybe the UK would discover something else to be proud about.

GREAT IDEAS TIED UP IN RED TAPE

The government does want to help, but it struggles to understand what a small business owner's life is really like. My business has very much welcomed initiatives like the Enterprise Management Incentive (EMI) and Research and Development (R&D) tax relief. However, implementing them has been tough. Take EMI: we want to be able to share our business's success with employees. The tax incentives make it attractive too. Yet the process does not. If we hadn't been utterly committed to the idea, we would have given up on EMI long ago. It's the same story with R&D tax relief. Through pragmatic advice from one of our accountants, we have learnt how to apply, the format in which to do it and so on. It will make a big difference to our tax bill.

Overall it sounds good, except that in both cases it has taken time and money to put these schemes in place. Legal and accountancy fees have mounted up and so has our frustration. Given how time-poor and financially stretched small businesses can be, government really needs to keep bureaucracy and complexity to a minimum, if it wants to see take up of incentives like these.

SETTING THE STAGE FOR GROWTH

The small businesses we work with every day could do with more. More incentives, more advice, more understanding and support.

I have loved watching how technical innovation has already transformed opportunities for small businesses and I am genuinely optimistic about what future iterations will bring. App development starts from business needs, and then delivers a solution that makes things easier. I'd really like to see the press adopt a similarly positive approach, and government too. I'd like to see a greater understanding of how challenging it can be to set up and run a small business, with support tailored accordingly. That way, high-growth SMEs will have a real opportunity to compete, not just with big businesses in the UK but also on an international stage.

John Davis is managing director of BCSG, a fast-growing firm offering cloud-based applications to small businesses.

IV

Business and Government Working Together for the Long Term

REBUILDING THE UK INDUSTRIAL BASE

Ha-Joon Chang and Antonio Andreoni

The structural weaknesses of the UK's industrial base can be over-come with three key policy options: upgrading the technological infrastructure in partnership with the private sector; encouraging long-term thinking, investment and shareholding in the financial sector; and addressing the serious skills gaps and mismatches.

Since the 2008 global financial crisis, there has been a widespread acceptance—even among many of the traditional proponents of the finance-led service economy—that the UK needs to rebalance its economy and engineer a new manufacturing renaissance. However, few people realise the scale of this challenge, given the longstanding structural problems affecting the UK national industrial system. Also, the widespread scepticism about the possibility of the government partnering with productive companies to transform national productive capabilities has made policy responses slow, poorly co-ordinated and ineffective.

Until the end of the 19th century, the UK dominated the global industrial landscape. In 1860, it produced 20% of world manufacturing output. In 1870, it accounted for 46% of world trade in manufactured goods. The scale of the UK's then industrial dominance can be put into perspective by recalling that currently the share of China, the new "workshop of the world," in world manufacturing exports is only around 17% (as of 2012).

Over the last half-century, especially after 1970, the UK industrial base has been diminished, not just in its scale relative to the economy but also in its degree of diversification. The advanced manufacturing activities remaining in the UK today are concentrated in three sectors—namely, automotive, aerospace and life sciences. Between 1997 and 2007, only aerospace and pharmaceuticals registered a sustained GVA (gross value added) growth, although the pharmaceutical industry has entered a profound contraction cycle since 2007.[1] These three and other "advanced manufacturing" industries (such as nuclear energy and offshore wind) may account for only 4% of the UK's GDP, but they provide two thirds of all manufacturing business R&D and almost one third of total export.

Outside of these advanced manufacturing sectors, critical manufacturing competences have been lost and domestic supply chains have become highly fragmented. Moreover, even the few sectors in which the UK still excels internationally rely on relatively few companies, whose activities are concentrated in few regions. More importantly, their supply chains are rather globalised, including in the important area of knowledge-intensive producer inputs, such as production technologies and complex sub-system components.

The best evidence of the structural weakness of the UK national industrial system is given by the missed manufacturing export boom after 2008, despite a 30–35% devaluation of sterling. The UK industrial sector did not witness a significant production expansion even with a reduction of one third of the prices of its export goods. This shows that, without rebuilding the industrial base, even macroeconomic policies become ineffective.

GLOBAL LANDSCAPE AND EMERGING CHALLENGES

Many of the challenges that the UK is facing today can also be found in other mature industrial economies. However, unlike the

UK, countries such as Germany, Japan or the US have more proactively used the opportunity offered by the financial crisis to address some of their structural problems and boost their industrial sectors. This has been done with a combination of demand-side stimulus packages and supply-side industrial policies.

Many of the industrial policies adopted by these countries are not new at all.[2] Indeed, they have never stopped adopting these policies—often they have simply re-labelled them as innovation or competition policies. In those countries, governments have continued to play an entrepreneurial role, in partnership with private-sector companies, in reducing critical cost factors such as energy and finance; creating and regulating markets; investing in long-term and highly uncertain technological endeavours; building technological and physical infrastructures; and investing in industrial skills development.

Over the last decade, emerging industrial economies like China, Brazil, India and Singapore have even strengthened their industrial policy packages to maintain the pace of manufacturing output growth and their penetration of the international manufacturing trade.[3] As a result, China was able to increase its shares in world manufactured trade from 4% to 17% over the period 2000–2010 (while the UK lost 2% of its shares), while building its technological and production capabilities. The increasing richness of these competences and the policy offering of these emerging countries have attracted not simply manufacturing plants but also R&D centres of major multinationals like IBM in China, DuPont in India and Rolls Royce in Singapore.[4]

These international manufacturing and policy trends are of critical importance for the UK for at least two reasons.

The first and the obvious reason is that the experiences of other countries show how rebuilding the UK industrial base is not simply a way for rebalancing the economy. More critically, it is a precondition for preserving the existing advanced manufacturing sectors and their R&D facilities, for attracting multinationals willing to invest in competences-rich industrial ecosystems and for making the

UK national industrial system more resilient and ready to capture future global market opportunities.

IS INDUSTRIAL POLICY NON-BRITISH?

Another, less often recognised, implication of the international diversity of industrial policy experiences is that there are many industrial policy measures, programmes and institutional solutions to draw on in rebuilding the UK industrial base. Learning from other countries in relation to any policy generates scepticism in all countries, but that reaction is particularly strong when it comes to industrial policy in the UK. Industrial policy, it is often argued, however successful it may have been in other countries, is against the country's history of *laissez-faire* capitalism and its tradition of individualism.

One problem with this view is that it is based on a mistaken view of British history. Between the industrial policy reform of Robert Walpole in 1721 until the transition to free trade in the 1860s, Britain was in fact the pioneer of industrial policy. It is because he knew this history that Friedrich List, the 19th-century German economist who is mistakenly known as the father of the infant industry argument (the real father is Alexander Hamilton, the first US Treasury Secretary), wrote in the 1840s that Britain's preaching of free trade to then economically backwards nations, like Germany and the US, was like "kicking away the ladder."[5] In turn, Alexander Hamilton is known to have drawn inspirations from Walpole's policies in developing his infant industry argument, so much so that he was accused of being a "Walpolean" by his opponents who did not share his belief in government intervention. So, it is a convenient myth for the opponents of industrial policy that industrial policy is against the British tradition, when one could argue that Britain actually first invented it.

All the success cases of industrial policy are countries that have actively learnt from the more successful countries in terms of policy traditions, institutional set-ups and culture. Just to cite some prominent examples, in the 18th and early 19th centuries, the US and Germany learnt from Britain's industrial policy; in the late 19th century, Japan imported a lot of policies and institutions from Germany; in the 20th century, Korea and China have aggressively learnt from Japan.

The first important step in the revival of industrial policy in the UK is thus changing the negative perception around it. Without this change, the UK government would not be open to learning from the successes as well as the failures of other countries in the area of industrial policy and whichever industrial policy measures that it adopts will not become integral parts of the government agenda, resulting in policy misalignment that reduces the effectiveness of those measures.

MISUNDERSTANDING MODERN MANUFACTURING INDUSTRIES

The negative perception of industrial policy in the UK has been reinforced by the misunderstanding of modern manufacturing industries. Manufacturing industries have witnessed a dramatic transformation over the last few decades, which, in spite of the dominant vision, have indeed increased their strategic relevance for even service-led economies like the UK.

Modern manufacturing companies orchestrate production processes through complex producer networks spanning across the globe, as well as across different industrial sectors. Not only have they become vertically more disintegrated, they have also reached higher levels of flexibility in production processes and higher degrees of customisation in product design. As a result, manufacturing products have become "systems" whose production requires the integration of different manufacturing sub-systems as well as the deployment of an array of sophisticated producer services. This, in turn, means that manufactured products are in fact critical vehicles for exporting knowledge-intensive business services in which the UK has developed a distinctive competitive advantage.

The technological capabilities that underpin these complex manufacturing processes are owned by companies of different sizes and operate at different links in different global value chains. Many of these companies often work across different sectors, supplying different value chains with similar technical solutions and components. This cross-cutting nature of manufacturing capabilities also means that mature manufacturing companies can start a new life in new sectors by applying some of their existing capabilities to different sectors and products. Given this, sectoral policies focusing on particular sectors should be complemented by cross-sectoral measures and better aligned to technology policies. These cross-sectoral measures include investments in technologies whose applicability span across industries, such as advanced materials and robotics.

Appreciating the systemic nature of the economy also means that companies cannot be seen in isolation. For example, when some big companies with deep roots in the UK (here we are not merely talking about the legal ownership status, as in the case of Astra Zeneca) are taken over by foreign companies, it can lead to the disruption of the entire supply chain of SMEs and even the impoverishment of the industrial ecosystem around it, including their relationships with universities and local research centres.

The systemic perspective also means that government policies towards small and medium-sized enterprises (SMEs) should not be conceived simply in terms of their size status. An un-differentiated support for SMEs would ignore the critical role that knowledge-intensive small companies and specialist contractors play in value creation and in attracting foreign investments. The regional industrial ecosystem around Cambridge is a good example.

NEW INDUSTRIAL POLICY OPTIONS FOR THE UK

Given the above considerations, what are the industrial policy options for the UK? Not denying the value of the "traditional" sectoral industrial policy measures intended to encourage upgrading at the sectoral level, we would like to highlight the importance of industrial policy measures intended to upgrade the "industrial infrastructure" of the UK economy. The focus on industrial infrastructure means that industrial policy will require, more than before, the coordination between different specialised agencies, particularly the Business, Innovation and Skills (BIS) Department and the Technology Strategy Board (TSB), but also other central government departments and local government institutions, like the Local Enterprise Partnerships (LEPs).

That the UK requires a serious upgrading of the physical infrastructure is widely accepted. Far less recognised is the need to upgrade the technological infrastructure—that is, the tissue of institutions and organisations that encourage technological progress. This infrastructure is made up of institutions and organisations that facilitate the sharing of knowledge (e.g., public agencies funding pre-commercial research), the spreading of knowledge (e.g., "extension services" for SMEs) and the cross-fertilisation of knowledge across industrial sectors and different actors (e.g., public and semi-public agencies facilitating collaboration in innovation between firms, universities and government agencies).

And indeed, many competitor countries to the UK are building a better technological infrastructure. In the US, the National Network for Manufacturing Innovation (NNMI) and the Manufacturing Extension Partnerships (MEP) are getting technologies to SMEs, support the adoption of new organisational models and help companies in scaling up their production. Fraunhofer Institutes in Germany are even more effective and comprehensive in their roles, not least thanks to an annual budget almost four times bigger than that of its UK counterpart, TSB. Even some emerging economies have built impressive public-private R&D institutions, like the agro-tech institutional network EMBRAPA in Brazil. EMBRAPA's success has been such that its model has been recently imported into the UK.

To enable the upgrading of technological infrastructure, the UK's financial infrastructure needs to be redesigned. The UK financial institutions are too much driven by short-termist incentives, hampering investments in technologies that will bear fruits only in the long run.

The establishment of a development bank with a longer time horizon (five years instead of one, to put it crudely) is one solution that has been used to encourage long-term investments in many countries, including Germany (KfW), Japan (JDB), Korea (KDB) and Brazil (BNDES). Indeed, this option has been frequently discussed in the UK, most notably by Lord Robert Skidelsky, for the development bank set up by the current government (the British Business Bank).[6] Unfortunately, the BBB is insufficiently focused on manufacturing industries, which need longer-term finance for technological development than any other sector does.[7]

Another idea is to induce banks to lend more to productive enterprises by tightening the regulations on consumer loans and housing loans. This measure will have an added benefit of dampening the inherent tendency of the UK financial system to create financial bubbles, especially property bubbles. Of course, the difficulty here is that in the recent period the UK banks have lost the ability to assess, discriminate and evaluate the risk (and potential future returns) of industrial projects. This means that there is a need for a significant re-tooling of loan officers in the banking industry. This will take time, but at least it can be kick-started in the two major banks in public ownership—RBS and HBOS.

Furthermore, we can introduce measures to encourage long-term shareholding. Some people accept the need for this but are sceptical regarding its feasibility in the UK, given the inherently shareholder-oriented nature of its financial system. However, we believe that some of this can be achieved even without fundamental institutional re-designs, like the introduction of a co-determination system like in Germany. For example, longer-term shareholding can be encouraged even within the current UK system by measures like graduated reduction in capital gains tax according to the period of shareholding or conferring of more votes to shares held over a longer period.

Last but not least, the UK needs an upgrading of its infrastructure-producing skills. It is widely agreed that the UK suffers from serious gaps and mismatches in skills, which are hindering the country's firms' capacities for transforming and translating research outputs (which are exceptionally high by international standards) into industrial activities at the shop floor level.[8] The challenge is huge if we consider that UK companies are projected to need 1.86 million people with engineering skills between 2010 and 2020. However, a lot of useful lessons can be learned from other countries that have been more successful in this respect—Germany's integrated vocational training system or the Scandinavian system of re-skilling and continuous education.

NEW INDUSTRIAL PARTNERSHIPS

The structural weaknesses of the UK's industrial base call for effective industrial policy by its government. However, this does not mean going back to the 1960s or the 1970s—the last time the UK tried industrial policy. The policy measures need to take into account recent changes, such as the changed structure of the UK manufacturing sector and the rise of global value chains. Moreover, in order to be effective, the UK's new industrial policy measures have to be better coordinated than they are now. For the UK, the most important step is the re-building of the country's industrial infrastructure in partnership with the private sector—not only with those manufacturing companies that are currently playing a pivotal role in the industrial sector but also with all the companies that are willing to share the risks and the gains of a systemic industrial restructuring of the UK economy.

Ha-Joon Chang teaches economics at Cambridge University and writes a column for the *Guardian*. His last book, *Economics: The User's Guide*, was published by Penguin.

Antonio Andreoni is a researcher in industrial economics and policy at the Institute for Manufacturing, Cambridge University, and coordinator of the Babbage Industrial Policy Network.

NOTES

1. BIS Growth Dashboard, 2014.

2. O'Sullivan, E., Andreoni, A., Lopez, C. and Gregory, M. (2013) "What is New in the New Industrial Policy? A Manufacturing System Perspective," *Oxford Review of Economic Policy*, 29(2), 432–462.

3. Chang, H.-J., Andreoni, A. and Kuan, M. L. (2013) "International Industrial Policy Experiences and the Lessons for the UK," in *The Future of Manufacturing*, UK Government Office of Science, London: BIS.

4. Berger, S. (2013) *Making in America: From Innovation to Market*, Cambridge, MA: MIT.

5. Chang, H.-J. (2002) *Kicking Away the Ladder: Development Strategy in Historical Perspective*, London: Anthem Press.

6. British Business Bank (2014) Strategic Plan, London: BIS.

7. The same goes for other government lending and investment. Most notably, as of December 2013, only one-fifth of the 2.6bn allocated investments from the Regional Growth Fund established in 2010 reached productive businesses.

8. According to the *International Comparative Performance of the UK Research Base* Report commissioned by the BIS Department, the UK has a strong and highly productive research base, in terms of both articles and citation outputs per researcher. While the UK accounts for just 2.4% of global patents applications, the UK's share of citations from patents to journal articles is 10.9%.

SUPPORTING COMPANIES IN A SCALE-UP REVOLUTION

Sherry Coutu

In order to support the next generation of high-growth companies, it is vitally important that Britain move from being a great place to start firms to also being a great place to "scale up" firms.

Britain has come a long way since I emigrated here in the mid-1980s as a young, foreign student from a logging town in Canada on a scholarship to study at the London School of Economics. In stark contrast to when I set up my first business in 1994, it is now an outstanding place to start-up. As an angel investor, since floating and selling my own businesses, which were high-growth scale-ups, I have helped finance more than 50 others, which have operations in more than 70 countries, employ tens of thousands of people and turnover in excess of £3 billion.

Britain is, however, not yet an outstanding place to scale up a business. The good news is that it is relatively cheap and easy to become a "scale-up nation" and all the pieces that are needed to make this happen are largely already in place—but they are not currently targeted on supporting companies to grow rapidly.

OVERCOMING POLITICAL BIAS

Focusing on supporting companies which are already growing might not be popular, as one might hypothesise that supporting 500 one-person micro businesses is as good as supporting one business that grows its employees from 1 to 500. From the perspective of voters, the former may be preferable, but from an economic growth point of view, the wealth of academic research shows—beyond any doubt—that economic growth and national competitive advantage is tied to the success of high-growth scale-up firms. Although scale-ups play an important role in stimulating the economy, they also face many hurdles, especially in the UK, where they encounter a culture that seems biased towards established large firms and SMEs—neither of which are necessarily growing.

The responsibility to become a scale-up nation rests with all of us. Leaders of large companies, financial companies, the media, schools, universities and local and national policymakers all have a vital role to play. Individually and collectively, we can collaborate to co-create a future that is bright for our children and their children: a place where scale-ups flourish alongside start-ups. Concentrating on economic growth without regard for whether companies are large or small, shrinking or growing, feels like being in a crowded noisy room with the lights off. We need the government to turn on the lights and then we can concentrate on doing what we know will work.

THE JOBS OF THE FUTURE

It is vital that we prepare our children for the jobs that "will be" rather than those "that are" or, even worse, those "that were." 100% of the net new jobs created in Europe in the past five years were from companies less than five years old. At the same time, there are so many young people who are unemployed whilst these fast-growth young companies cite unavailability of appropriate skill sets—rather than regulation or taxation—as the number one barrier to being able to grow faster. Overcoming these hurdles at sufficient pace and scale to build sustainable competitive advantage is crucial in the fast-moving digital world. If nothing changes, many of these fast-growth ventures will continue to fail to grow beyond borders and will continue to be taken over by larger (often non-European) companies at a significant discount to their true potential value. We cannot and must not let this happen.

There are lots of examples of how we might go about fixing this problem right now. "Best practice" points to collaborations between government, business and educators that produce mind-boggling results in terms of job creation and customer order growth which cost very little: we should do lots more of these.

We should work together to create a strategy that produces the same number of jobs and turnover growth per scale-up company as international "best practice" examples have around the world. The industry structure, geographic placement and science base in the UK are poised to create unrivalled national competitive advantage if we now turn our focus to scaling up our most promising companies. Indeed, there are many reasons why we should be able to create even more jobs and revenue growth than other countries can muster.

THE NEED FOR A SCALE-UP REVIEW

I would urge us all to do a "scale-up review" of our initiatives, time spent and money spent trying to boost "economic growth" to ask two questions: First, are we doing enough to celebrate and support the scale-ups that are creating jobs now and those jobs that will be prevalent in five to ten years' time? Or might it be tilted towards celebrating "ideas and startups" or "big companies" regardless of whether those companies are growing or shrinking? Can you name the top 50 fastest-growing companies within 20 miles of you? Can you name the top 50 fastest-growing life-science companies? Can you name the top 50 fastest-growing manufacturing companies? Can you name the fastest-growing in terms of both revenue and employment in your county or country? Finding them is easy—they are all around us, and the Government collects all of this information already.

The Government releasing data on which companies are growing the fastest around us would be the single most empowering act. Rather than depend on others to "sell" or "give" data to investors, we could have access to it ourselves. How liberating! How democratic! At the moment, the data is not available—at any cost—even though a high cost has already been extracted from the companies that had to devote their resources to collating and submitting it to the Government, not to mention to creating the products that customers wanted in the first place. Investors need turnover figures that are up-to-date and employment figures for each company going back four years so we can spot which ones are growing.

Second, is the balance of our support sufficiently oriented towards ensuring the success of scale-ups? Bearing in mind that these companies state their number one hurdle as being access to skills and the number two hurdle as developing leaders with skills and experience to cope with the growth they are experiencing, if we looked at the amount spent or time devoted each week by each department or civil servant to removing barriers to growth for these companies, would the balance lie with microbusinesses or large corporates?

If we looked at the amount of services bought by local and central governments, would the lion's share of procurement be done with shrinking firms or growing firms? In the US, they ask government departments to report on the growth rate of the companies they procure services from in order to gauge how innovative they are being. Might we do the same? Sadly, at the moment, we cannot answer that question, as the data is not released to us in order to answer the questions for ourselves.

I would urge us all to adjust the portfolio of time and money we spend on boosting economic growth to focus on what scale-ups say they need most, which is firstly talent, and then customers, followed by finance, infrastructure and tax breaks.

Why look at employment figures for scale-ups? Because jobs are important! Why look at turnover figures in the past three years for scale-ups? Because turnover is an important measure of customers buying products that are valuable to them. If turnover is increasing, it is a great way to tell that the products being sold are innovative and worth having. These are the leading indicators that need light shined upon them.

Acting together, we can boost jobs and growth in the next one, five and ten years' time, and I look forward to helping make that happen. My guess is that this could easily put an additional £100 billion onto the "bottom line" of our economic growth and that the cost of achieving this is in the tens of millions.

Sherry Coutu CBE is an angel investor and serves on the boards of companies, charities and universities.

THE POWER OF TECHNOLOGY CLUSTERS

David Cleevely

There are significant lessons from the Cambridge success story: the city is arguably the most successful technology cluster in the UK, with £13 billion revenue from high-tech and a Gross Value Added per job of £54,000 (40% higher than London).

Innovation drives productivity and economic growth, so it is unsurprising that successive UK Governments have promoted innovation. On many measures the UK's performance is impressive—for example, third place in the recent Global Innovation Index (behind Switzerland and Sweden and ahead of the US).

But our everyday experiences tell us something different: we see many innovative products, services and processes to improve productivity that come from abroad. It is often said that the UK has great ideas but cannot commercialise them. There is a strong sense that we need to do more to promote innovation.

Of course, we should be careful about creating new policies. This is a marathon, not a sprint: policy continuity through institutions such as the TSB and the Catapults (formerly Technology Innovation Centres) has served the UK well. Nevertheless, we need to look carefully at what is working and scale that up, and identify what isn't working and needs to be changed.

LESSONS FROM A CAMBRIDGE SUCCESS STORY

First an apology. This analysis is based on my own experience. I live and work mostly in Cambridge. Despite its relatively small size, in the last 15 years Cambridge has generated 14 companies worth over $1 billion, two of which are worth over $10 billion. It is home to not only 90 Nobel Prizes but also the world's most successful blockbuster drug (Humira) and ARM, the revenue from whose chips is greater than Intel. With £13 billion in revenue from high-tech and Cambridge enjoying a Gross Value Added per job of £54,000 (40% higher than London), it is arguably the most successful technology cluster in the United Kingdom.

Back in 2004, I co-founded a company called 3WayNetworks to make 3G mini cellular base stations—the kind of thing Vodafone sells now as Sure Signal. We brought together individuals who had had previous experience in working together. Many of the team members were frustrated in their existing large organisations, where the pace of innovation was relatively slow. The company received funding from Cambridge Angels—entrepreneurs who themselves had made money from successful exits. The networks in Cambridge made it relatively easy to get resources such as accommodation, new recruits, advice, financial support and introductions to key players globally—especially in the US, which rapidly became our biggest market.

In February 2007, three things happened which, within a few weeks, would lead us to sell to Airvana, a US firm looking for novel technology to bolster its upcoming listing on NASDAQ. First, the mobile operator who wanted to buy 5,000 units said it could only do so through one of 5 approved suppliers. Second, the mobile world congress in Barcelona that year had 12 competing technologies on show—up from 1 the year before. Third, the amount we would add to the US firm's value at IPO was far bigger than the sale price we would accept.

It was right to sell the company. Even the last investors to join made 3 times their money in 18 months. The team in Cambridge grew rapidly and made great progress. Then Airvana was taken private, the office closed down and the team dispersed. Team members went on to form or join other companies and have subsequently developed other products or patents funded in part by the money made from the sale. Airvana took the technology to the US and recently added 4G base stations to its product line.

This single example sums up many of the things that I have seen over the last 30 years or so. I want to draw on from it 5 simple policy recommendations.

BUY FROM SMEs

Most innovation policies focus on the supply side. But early sales are worth more than investment. 3WayNetworks had an innovative product, and there were specialist customers who were prepared to pay for it well before it had been developed to the point where it could be sold to a mass market. Developing, making and supplying those few hundred units taught us more about the final product than we could have learnt burning through millions of VC money.

More needs to be done to encourage and enable large organisations—both government and private—to buy from SMEs. Procurement needs to be encouraged to get smarter, not just treated as a risk minimisation exercise where everything ought to be bought at the lowest possible price. The UK has programmes, but they are miniscule compared to the US, where government has very high targets for buying from SMEs.

Hence my first recommendation is to buy more from fast-growing, small, innovative companies. The actual money spent on procurement from SMEs by both government and by the suppliers to government should be made public—and, when procuring from large companies, their historical track record of purchasing from

SMEs should be given significant weight in deciding between suppliers. We should benchmark ourselves against the US. We should break contracts up into smaller components so SMEs can participate and have parallel competing projects in the early stages prior to scaling up.

MAKE INNOVATION PART OF REGULATION

Only two of the UK's nine economic regulators (Ofcom and the FCA) have innovation as part of their duties—and judging from their web sites, neither has thought fit to publicise this. Regulators all focus on competition and consumer issues, decisions are taken on narrowly defined cost benefit analyses and consultation is used as a mechanism for checking and ratifying proposals.

Of course, competition is a driver of innovation, and consumers need a good deal. However, innovation should have greater weight in decisions because that is what drives economic growth in the long run.

Taking decisions based on narrow cost-benefit analysis begs the question of what are the costs and benefits. No CEO of an innovative company would rely on his or her CFO to have the final say in what should or should not be done—and there is plenty of evidence from companies like Kodak of what happens when short-term financial consideration outweighs longer-term strategy.

Consultation too often means listening to large companies that can lobby effectively because they can afford to. It is a process which appears open but is in fact biased. With most job creations and economic growth coming from a tiny fraction of fast-growing innovative SMEs, this is a major issue. These regulators set the rules for a very large proportion of our economy: they should be required to promote innovation and to take the impact on innovation into account.

My second recommendation is therefore to make innovation part of regulation. The 9 UK economic regulators should be instructed to promote innovation. Engineering expertise (especially from fast-growing SMEs) should be included alongside economic considerations when making decisions. Fast-growing SMEs should be brought into the consultation process through workshops and other forms of active engagement.

FREE UP UNIVERSITY INTELLECTUAL PROPERTY

We should be wary of the apparently obvious. Technology transfer and the role of universities in R&D are frequently held up as sources of innovation. Whilst true to some extent, these play a relatively minor role. They manage to get a lot of attention thanks to their visibility and successful lobbying.

The real source of growth is companies founded by alumni. The Computer Lab at the University of Cambridge boasts 222 companies in its hall of fame, including Deep Mind and ARM, and their total market value is many tens of billions of pounds. The Computer Lab—and indeed the whole University—has a relaxed attitude to Intellectual Property; its alumni go on to create great companies and donations exceed IP license revenue. This is in sharp contrast to most policies on technology transfer which emphasise Universities owning IP—one start up recently reported to me that their University wanted 60% of their company, with the result that they are not going ahead with the plan as originally proposed.

Attempts to claim large chunks of value only results in that value evaporating. But there is another way—as proposed by Hermann Hauser, Andy Hopper and myself. Free up University IP by enabling the Golden Share: alumni who are company founders should be able to donate a non-dilutable 2%. This should be made legally binding and watertight. The result will be more money for Universities. In the case of the Computer Lab, it would have yielded hundreds of millions—far more than any money raised by tech transfer and comparable with any of the largest University-wide fund raising campaigns.

MORE SUPPORT FOR CLUSTERS

According to Bengt-Åke Lundvall, a national system of innovation is cumulative (so success builds on success), non-linear (so doubling the input won't double the output) and path dependent (so where you have come from determines what happens next), and it continuously learns from what it does.

None of these is susceptible to an easy policy fix. We need to appreciate that a national system of innovation is a system of networks that operate at and between many levels from the individual up to the state. The actors in the system have multiple motivations: competition and profit, creation, discovery and working with others to achieve seemingly impossible goals.

As the Cambridge model shows, a national system of innovation can only operate through local clusters where the travel time is under an hour; where people and ideas mix freely and where there are role models; where there are local (recycled) capital, great events, universities, champions, local press, alumni, local wins, second-time entrepreneurs and "marquee" local companies (as noted by Suster and Feld).

We have yet to develop a consistent cluster policy in the UK. Lord Heseltine's Report in 2013 with its emphasis on localism, the recent Centre for Cities report and the Adonis Review have paved the way forward. Nevertheless, we need to recognise that these clusters grow from the ground up and, where they exist, they need support. Infrastructure and investment will not be sufficient. We need to help local leaders and entrepreneurs in their ambition to build the local networks and governance which will generate the innovation and growth.

The missing policy key to a national system of innovation is local clusters. Direct financial support to privately led networks could be provided by commissioning work and events from them. Clusters should benefit from the appropriate local government structure (this means unitary authorities). They should be incentivised to work together to share best practice.

FAST BROADBAND EVERYWHERE

Finally, fast broadband—fixed and mobile—should be made available everywhere. Broadband is one of the General Purpose Technologies, along with the wheel, writing, printing and perhaps 20 or so others, invented by mankind. It enables participation in the modern economy—for both suppliers and consumers—and (as has been shown by the growth of companies like Google) has been the platform on which huge new industries have been built.

To sum up, we have tax incentives, catapults, the TSB and a whole host of other initiatives. Now we need to engage with fast-growing SMEs and to understand and support them. We need to include innovation as one of the objectives when regulating sectors. We should be less obsessed with tech transfer and pay more attention to motivating the innovators. We need fast broadband available everywhere. But if I were to pick one single recommendation to make the UK even more innovative, it would be to learn from and develop its already hugely successful clusters.

David Cleevely CBE is an entrepreneur who has founded a series of companies, including Abcam, Analysys, 3waynetworks and others. He also co-founded Cambridge Network, Cambridge Wireless, Cambridge Angels and the award-winning restaurant Bocca di Lupo, as well as acting as government advisor and founding the Centre for Science and Policy at the University of Cambridge.